THE UX-PM CONNECTION

Bridging Design Usability & Business Goals

CHIDINMA EGBU

copyright © 2021 Chidinma Egbu All rights reserved

No part of this book may be reproduced or used in any manner without the author's written permission, except for brief quotations in book reviews.

Published by:
Emphaloz Publishing House
www.emphaloz.com

ISBN: 978-1-2589-8479-3

Printed in Nigeria

Great products don't succeed by accident, they are the result of a seamless collaboration between product management and UX. When strategy meets design, usability aligns with business goals, and user needs to drive decision-making, innovation thrives. The true power of product management lies in bridging vision and execution, ensuring that every feature delivers both value and impact."

TABLE OF CONTENTS

Foreword   v
Introduction   vii
Chapter 1
   The Ux-Pm Partnership Understanding The Two Worlds   1
Chapter 2
   Understanding The Ux Landscape   14
Chapter 3
   Decoding The Product Management Role A Comprehensive Exploration   35
Chapter 4
   Aligning Ux And Business Goals A Symbiotic Relationship For Sustainable Success   42
Chapter 5
   User Research: The Foundation Of Ux And Pm   50
Chapter 6
   Collaboration Strategies For Ux And Pm   56
Chapter 7
   Product Roadmaps And Prioritization   74
Chapter 8
   Measuring Ux Success And Roi   87
Chapter 9
   Case Studies Ux-Pm Collaboration In Action   98
Chapter 10
   The Future Of Ux-Pm Partnership: Navigating The Next Frontier   103

Foreword

In today's fast-paced digital landscape, the success of a product is no longer determined by functionality alone—it hinges on how seamlessly it integrates into users' lives. As organizations strive to create meaningful and engaging experiences, the collaboration between User Experience (UX) professionals and Product Managers (PMs) has never been more crucial. Yet, despite their shared goal of delivering value, these two disciplines often operate in silos, leading to misaligned priorities and missed opportunities.

The UX-PM Connection: Bridging Design, Usability, and Business Goals is a much-needed guide that brings clarity to this relationship, offering a strategic framework for collaboration. It unpacks the challenges that arise when UX and product management are not in sync and provides actionable insights to foster alignment. By bridging the gap between user-centric design and business objectives, organizations can build products that not only meet user needs but also drive measurable success.

This book serves as both a roadmap and a call to action for professionals seeking to create high-impact products. Whether you are a UX designer looking to better understand business constraints or a product manager aiming to integrate UX principles into your strategy, the insights within these pages will empower you to work more effectively, communicate more clearly, and ultimately, build better products.

It is time to move beyond the debate of UX vs. PM and embrace the synergy that comes from their partnership. This book will show you how.

Introduction

In today's fiercely competitive market, where users are bombarded with choices and their expectations are constantly rising, creating successful products is more challenging than ever. It's no longer enough to simply have a functional product; it must be intuitive, enjoyable, and seamlessly integrated into users' lives. This is where the powerful synergy between User Experience (UX) and Product Management (PM) becomes paramount. This book, "The UX-PM Connection," is a guide to understanding, fostering, and leveraging this critical partnership to build products that not only meet business objectives but also delight and engage users.

For too long, UX and Product Management have often operated in silos, leading to misaligned priorities, missed opportunities, and ultimately, products that fall short of their potential. UX teams, focused on crafting exceptional user experiences, sometimes struggle to translate their user-centric vision into tangible product features that align with business goals. Product Managers, tasked with defining product strategy and driving execution, may prioritize features based on market trends or technical feasibility, inadvertently overlooking the crucial role of user needs and usability. This disconnect can result in products that are technically sound but fail to resonate with their target audience, leading to low adoption rates, negative user feedback, and ultimately, a missed opportunity for market success.

This book aims to bridge this gap by illuminating the symbiotic relationship between UX and PM. It argues that when UX and PM work in close collaboration, they form an unstoppable force capable of creating truly exceptional products. This book is not just for UX designers or product managers; it's for anyone involved in the product development process, from developers and marketers to business leaders and entrepreneurs. It provides a comprehensive framework for understanding the roles and responsibilities of both UX and PM, fostering effective communication, and aligning their efforts to achieve shared goals.

We will explore the core principles of user-centered design, delve into the intricacies of product strategy, and examine the crucial role of user research in informing product decisions. This book will equip you with the knowledge and tools necessary to:

Understand the distinct yet intertwined roles of UX and PM: We will dissect the responsibilities of each discipline, highlight their unique contributions and demonstrate how they complement each other.

Foster effective collaboration between UX and PM teams: We will provide practical strategies for building strong working relationships, fostering open communication, and establishing shared goals.

Align UX efforts with business objectives: We will explore how to translate user needs into tangible product features that drive business growth and achieve strategic objectives.

Leverage user research to inform product decisions: We will delve into various user research methodologies, demonstrating how user insights can validate design choices and drive product innovation.

Measure the success of UX initiatives and demonstrate ROI: We will explore key UX metrics and guide tracking and analyzing data to demonstrate the value of UX to stakeholders.

Throughout this book, we will draw upon real-world examples, case studies, and best practices to illustrate the power of the UX-PM partnership. We will examine how leading companies have successfully integrated UX and product management to create groundbreaking products that have disrupted markets and delighted users. These practical examples will provide you with tangible takeaways that you can implement in your work.

Establishing the UX-PM connection is possible, welcome to the roadmap of symbiotic partnership.

CHAPTER 1
THE UX-PM PARTNERSHIP
UNDERSTANDING THE TWO WORLDS

User Experience design fundamentally revolves around human-centered approaches to product creation. UX designers are champions of the end user, employing empathy, research, and design thinking to create intuitive, engaging, and valuable experiences. Their north star is user satisfaction and the emotional connection between people and products.

The UX practitioner's toolkit includes user research methods, persona development, journey mapping, information architecture, interaction design, wireframing, prototyping, visual design, UI pattern libraries, accessibility principles, and usability evaluation techniques. UX designers typically operate in iterative cycles, embracing ambiguity as part of the creative process. They value exploration, experimentation, and the freedom to pivot based on user feedback.

Product Managers, by contrast, are orchestrators of value creation. They define product strategy, prioritize features, and coordinate across disciplines to ensure products solve real customer problems while achieving business objectives. Their focus centers on market fit, business viability, and the strategic evolution of the product. The Product Manager's arsenal includes market research, competitive analysis, business modeling, feature prioritization frameworks, product road mapping, stakeholder alignment, go-to-market planning, and success metrics. PMs typically balance both strategic vision and tactical execution, making decisions that optimize for both short-term wins and long-term product health. They value evidence-based decision-making, market validation, and measurable outcomes.

These fundamental differences in orientation create an inherent tension between UX and product management disciplines:

UX Design Values	Product Management Values
User-centered	Market-centered
Experience quality	Business viability
Design thinking	Strategic thinking
Problem finding	Problem prioritization
Depth of solution	Breadth of impact
Emotional connection	Market differentiation

This tension, while challenging, isn't inherently negative. It creates a productive equilibrium that can drive innovation while maintaining sustainable product development. The key lies in acknowledging these differences while finding common ground to build upon.

The Evolution of Collaboration

The relationship between UX design and product management has evolved significantly over the past few decades. In traditional product development environments, designers often operated as service providers to product managers, brought in to "make things pretty" after core product decisions had already been made. Product managers, meanwhile, frequently make assumptions about user needs without the benefit of robust research.

As a methodology, Professor Robert Steinhauser noted in his seminal work on cross-discipline collaboration: "The historical separation between user advocacy and business advocacy stems not from personality conflicts but from systemic misalignment of incentives and mental models."

The rise of digital products in the early 2000s began to shift this paradigm. With increased competition and user expectations, the importance of thoughtful user experience became impossible to ignore. Meanwhile, the emergence of design thinking as a problem-solving approach created a common language between UX and product management.

The subsequent popularization of lean product development, customer development, and jobs-to-be-done frameworks further evolved the landscape. These methodologies emphasized validated learning, user insight, and cross-functional collaboration—creating more natural integration points between UX and product management disciplines.

Today's most successful organizations have progressed beyond mere tolerance between these functions to active cultivation of their partnership. They recognize that neither discipline in isolation can deliver optimal outcomes in the complex digital product landscape.

The Value of Partnership

When UX designers and Product Managers collaborate effectively, organizations realize numerous tangible benefits. Research by the Product Development Consortium found that organizations with high UX-PM collaboration scores launched products with 42% higher customer satisfaction and reported 37% better revenue performance compared to organizations where these functions operated in silos.

These benefits manifest in several keyways:

Market-Driven Innovation: The integration of user needs with market opportunities creates products that are both desirable to users and viable in the marketplace.

Decision Quality: Collaborative teams make better-informed product decisions by combining user insights with business constraints and strategic direction.

Focused Execution: Aligned UX-PM teams create clearer direction for development teams, reducing wasted effort and increasing the likelihood of building the right features.

Reduced Time-to-Value: By integrating user feedback earlier and more continuously in the development process, teams avoid building features that users don't want or can't use.

Strategic Alignment: A unified UX-PM front creates clearer, more compelling narratives about product direction, reducing stakeholder misalignment and scope creep.

Beyond organizational gains, end users benefit substantially from strong UX-PM collaboration. They receive products that not only address their needs but remain sustainable and continuously improving because they're built on sound business models. They experience more cohesive product experiences, better-prioritized features that address their most critical pain points, and transparent communication about product evolution.

Foundations of Effective Partnership

At the foundation of every successful UX-PM partnership lies a set of shared mental models—common understandings of problems, opportunities, and priorities that enable coordinated action despite different disciplinary perspectives.

These shared models typically include a mutual understanding of target users and their needs, product vision and strategy, value propositions, competitive landscape, and decision frameworks. Developing these shared models requires deliberate effort and ongoing maintenance through regular workshops, documentation practices, and cross-training opportunities.

Effective UX-PM partnerships also leverage the distinct yet complementary capabilities each role brings to product development. UX designers contribute deep user empathy, creative problem-solving approaches, visual communication skills, systems thinking, and qualitative research methodologies. Product managers bring market insight, strategic vision, prioritization frameworks, business acumen, and stakeholder alignment skills.

When these capabilities are recognized and integrated, teams can address challenges more holistically. For example, a UX designer's insight into a critical user pain point can be effectively prioritized through a PM's understanding of market opportunities and business impact.

Perhaps the most critical element of successful partnerships is establishing robust communication bridges between UX and product management functions. These bridges include shared vocabulary, translation protocols between different types of artifacts, regular feedback loops, conflict resolution mechanisms, and aligned documentation standards.

The most advanced teams move beyond basic communication to true integration, with hybrid artifacts and processes that simultaneously address both UX and PM concerns.

Patterns of Dysfunction

Despite the clear value of strong UX-PM partnerships, many organizations struggle to realize this potential. Several dysfunctional patterns recur across industries, undermining effective collaboration. In the common "handoff trap," UX work is treated as a service request that comes after product decisions have already been made. Product managers define features based primarily on business needs or stakeholder requests, then engage designers to "make it usable." This approach fails to leverage user insights during problem definition, encourages superficial design solutions, and prevents the creation of truly differentiated user experiences.

The "competing advocate problem" occurs when UX and PM functions position themselves as competing advocates from different perspectives. UX practitioners become single-minded champions of the user without considering business constraints, while PMs focus exclusively on business metrics without acknowledging user needs. This creates unnecessary opposition when in reality both perspectives are essential to product success.

In some organizations, UX and PM functions become siloed experts with little understanding of each other's domains—the "knowledge gap scenario." UX teams lack business context for their design decisions, while product teams make assumptions about users without research validation. This manifests as designers creating beautiful but impractical solutions, PMs defining features users don't want, and both sides becoming frustrated by perceived irrationality from the other.

Building a Framework for Collaboration

Overcoming these dysfunctions requires intentional effort to build structured collaboration between UX and PM functions. Effective partnerships begin with integrated discovery processes that blend user research with market analysis. Successful teams conduct joint user interviews, analyze competitive products together, and develop shared artifacts like persona/market fit matrices that connect user needs with business opportunities.

Rather than separating "design thinking" from "product thinking," effective organizations create unified product development processes that integrate both perspectives. They develop shared discovery rituals, collaborative prioritization frameworks, joint decision-making protocols, and integrated success metrics that blend user and business outcomes.

Long-term partnership success requires ongoing investment in capability building through reciprocal skill development, shared tools proficiency, cross-mentoring programs, and collaborative case studies. Product managers learn research moderation and design thinking methods, while UX practitioners gain exposure to business modeling and market analysis. Perhaps most importantly, organizations must align how they measure and reward UX and PM contributions through balanced scorecards, joint accountability, collaborative performance reviews, and celebration of partnership successes.

Success Stories

Fintech startup Wealth Wave struggled with the low adoption of their investment platform despite strong technical functionality. Market research showed demand, but users weren't engaging with the product as expected.

In 2022, the organization implemented a new approach centered on the UX-PM partnership. They created a dedicated "Investment Experience Squad" with co-leadership from senior UX and PM practitioners. Together they conducted contextual inquiry with target users, revealing that while the product's features were technically sound, the complex investment concepts created emotional barriers to adoption.

The UX-PM team developed a shared "confidence journey" that mapped how users progressed from financial uncertainty to investment confidence. This journey became both a design framework and a product roadmap, guiding feature prioritization and interface decisions with a dual focus on emotional experience and business outcomes.

The results were transformative: new user activation increased by 34%, average portfolio size grew by 28%, and referral rates doubled. Key lessons included the power of emotional insight combined with business metrics, the importance of shared prioritization frameworks, and the value of measuring both experience quality and business outcomes.

Enterprise SaaS company DataSphere faced challenges with its analytics platform. Product managers were successfully selling to executive buyers, but user adoption within client organizations remained low, threatening renewal rates.

Their solution was a comprehensive redesign of the UX-PM relationship. They implemented "dual discovery" sessions where UX and PM team members jointly interviewed both executive buyers and end users. They created a collaborative "value mapping" process that connected executive priorities to user workflows. Most importantly, they revised their success metrics to include both sales conversion and user adoption rates.

Over 12 months, this approach allowed Datasphere to maintain strong sales while increasing user adoption by 67% and reducing support tickets by 41%. Customer renewal rates improved from 78% to 92%. The DataSphere case illustrates how thoughtful collaboration can align seemingly contradictory priorities—executive needs and end-user experience—through shared understanding and integrated approaches.

Practical Collaboration Tools

Several hybrid artifacts have proven particularly valuable for bridging UX and PM perspectives. Opportunity solution trees connect business opportunities with user problems and potential solutions. Dual-track roadmaps visualize both experience goals and feature milestones. Value proposition canvases integrate user needs, competitor analysis, and market differentiation. Research repositories make user insights accessible throughout the product development process.

Regular, structured interactions build the collaborative muscle between UX and PM functions. Problem-framing workshops jointly define challenges before jumping to solutions. Assumption mapping sessions identify and test critical assumptions about both user needs and market opportunities. Inspiration Tours examines competitive products from both user experience and business model perspectives. Paired stakeholder interviews build a shared understanding of organizational context.

Navigating Challenges

Perhaps the most persistent challenge in UX-PM partnerships is balancing short-term feature delivery with longer-term experience evolution. Successful teams address this through experience debt tracking, dedicated capacity for foundational UX work, experience-level objectives alongside feature-level milestones, and continuous education of stakeholders about experience investment value.

UX and PM teams often face different pressures from organizational stakeholders. Navigating these effectively requires unified narratives, joint stakeholder management, balanced advocacy where each discipline supports the other's priorities, and proactive expectation-setting workshops.

As organizations grow, maintaining effective UX-PM partnerships becomes increasingly challenging. Strategies for scaling include documenting core collaboration principles, creating cross-functional centers of excellence, identifying partnership ambassadors, and establishing communities of practice that bring together UX and PM professionals.

The Future of Collaboration

Several trends are shaping the evolution of UX-PM partnerships. The rise of product-led growth models has elevated the importance of seamless user experience as a critical business driver. Advanced teams are adopting continuous discovery practices that blend UX research with market validation. Outcome-driven product development helps align priorities around common goals. The growing emphasis on design systems creates new collaboration opportunities around product consistency and scalability.

As digital products become increasingly complex and user expectations continue to rise, the importance of effective UX-PM partnerships will only grow. Organizations that invest in building these collaborative capabilities will gain significant competitive advantage through experience differentiation, market responsiveness, innovation velocity, and talent attraction and retention.

The partnership between UX designers and Product Managers represents a critical foundation for successful digital product development. Though these disciplines approach product creation from different perspectives and with different priorities, their integration creates a powerful symbiosis that drives both user satisfaction and business success.

Building effective partnerships requires intentional effort—developing shared mental models, establishing integrated processes, creating collaborative artifacts, and aligning incentives. Organizations that make this investment reap substantial rewards in product quality, market differentiation, and business performance.

In the chapters that follow, we'll explore specific methodologies and tools that support this partnership throughout the product development lifecycle, from initial concept to continuous evolution. We'll examine how UX-PM collaboration manifests in different organizational contexts and how it adapts to diverse market challenges.

But the fundamental truth remains when user advocates and market strategists work in true partnership, products transcend the ordinary to deliver experiences that delight users while achieving business objectives. This symbiotic relationship, sometimes challenging but immensely rewarding, forms the bedrock of exceptional digital product creation in the modern age.

CHAPTER 2
UNDERSTANDING THE UX LANDSCAPE

User Experience (UX) has undeniably become a fundamental pillar of modern design, moving beyond a niche specialty to an essential element that dictates how users interact with products and services. successful product development. For product managers, understanding the UX landscape isn't just valuable, it's essential. This chapter explores the key principles, methodologies, and tools that define UX practice, providing product managers with the knowledge needed to effectively collaborate with UX professionals and advocate for user-centered approaches within their organizations.

The Foundation of User Experience

User experience as a discipline has roots that stretch back to early human factors research in the mid-20th century, but it wasn't until the digital revolution that UX emerged as a distinct field. Initially focused on making software more usable, UX has expanded to encompass the entirety of a user's interaction with a product, service, or company across multiple touchpoints and channels. What began as usability engineering has matured into a multifaceted discipline that blends psychology, design, business strategy, and technology. Today's UX practitioners consider not just functionality, but emotional responses, contextual factors, and the holistic journey users take when engaging with products. The evolution of UX reflects broader shifts in how businesses view their relationships with customers. In earlier decades, companies often centered their thinking on internal capabilities and operational efficiency. Products were designed from the inside out, with features determined primarily by what was technically feasible or organizationally convenient. The rise of UX coincided with—and helped drive—a fundamental reorientation toward customer-centricity. This shift recognized that sustainable success requires understanding and addressing customer needs, preferences, and pain points. Product development could no longer be driven solely by internal stakeholders or technical considerations.

For product managers, this evolution matters because user experience has become a primary differentiator in crowded markets. When features and functionalities are easily replicated, the quality of experience often determines which products succeed and which fail. Consider how companies like Apple and Airbnb have distinguished themselves not primarily through novel features but through thoughtfully crafted experiences that resonate with users on emotional as well as practical levels. Understanding this landscape allows product managers to make informed decisions about where to invest resources and how to position their products competitively.

At the heart of UX practice lies user-centered design (UCD)an approach that places users' needs, limitations, and preferences at the center of design and development processes. Rather than building products based on assumptions about what users might want, UCD practitioners engage directly with users throughout the product lifecycle. The fundamental principles of UCD include early and continuous user involvement, iterative design processes, holistic design considerations, and multidisciplinary collaboration.

UCD isn't merely a collection of techniques but represents a philosophical stance about how products should be created. It challenges the notion that designer's engineers or product managers can intuitively know what users need without systematic investigation. It questions the assumption that user preferences can be accurately predicted based on past behaviors or demographic data alone. It rejects the idea that elegant solutions can emerge from isolated expertise, instead embracing collaborative approaches that bring diverse perspectives to bear on complex problems.

For product managers, embracing UCD principles means shifting from feature-driven to user-driven roadmaps. It means making space for discovery and iteration, even when timelines are tight. It means becoming comfortable with ambiguity, recognizing that the right solution may not be immediately apparent and must emerge through engagement with users. This shift doesn't diminish the importance of business considerations or technical constraints; rather, it recasts them as essential factors to be balanced against user needs in pursuit of truly successful products.

The adoption of user-centered design approaches varies widely across organizations and industries. In some contexts, UCD has become firmly established as the default mode of operation, with robust processes and substantial resources dedicated to understanding and addressing user needs. In others, UCD principles may be acknowledged rhetorically but undermined in practice by organizational structures, incentive systems, or cultural factors that prioritize other considerations. Part of a product manager's challenge is navigating these organizational realities while advocating for appropriate user-centered approaches.

Research and Design Methodologies

User research forms the foundation of effective UX practice. Without research, designs are based on assumptions rather than evidence, often leading to products that miss the mark. UX research encompasses a range of methodologies for understanding user behaviors, needs, motivations, and pain points. Qualitative research methods provide depth and context. They include user interviews, contextual inquiry, focus groups, and diary studies. Quantitative research methods provide scale and measurability. They include surveys, analytics analysis, A/B testing, and eye-tracking studies.

Comparing Qualitative and Quantitative Research

The distinction between qualitative and quantitative research reflects different epistemological approaches to understanding user behavior.

Qualitative methods seek to understand the "why" behind user actions and preferences, uncovering motivations, mental models, and contextual factors that influence behavior.

Quantitative methods focus more on the "what" and "how many," providing statistical validity and identifying patterns across larger populations.

Neither approach is inherently superior; they answer different questions and complement each other when used thoughtfully.

For product managers, these research methodologies offer invaluable insights for decision-making. Customer interviews reveal unmet needs that might become new features. Usage analytics highlight which existing features deliver value and which don't. Usability tests identify friction points that, if addressed, could improve conversion rates or reduce support costs. Effective product managers don't need to become research experts, but they should understand when and why to employ different research methods. They should know what questions research can answer and what questions it can't. And they should be skilled at translating research findings into actionable product requirements.

The Emergence of Research Operations (ResearchOps)
Research operations (ResearchOps) have emerged as an important supporting function for systematic user research. ResearchOps focuses on standardizing processes, managing participant recruitment, maintaining research repositories, establishing ethical guidelines, and creating infrastructure that enables research to scale effectively across an organization. For product managers in larger organizations, familiarity with ResearchOps can help ensure that

research activities align with product development timelines and generate insights that can be leveraged beyond individual projects.

The timing and scope of user research deserve careful consideration. Traditional development approaches often front-loaded research into a distinct "requirements gathering" phase, but contemporary practices tend to distribute research activities throughout the product lifecycle. Discovery research helps identify opportunities before specific solutions are defined. Evaluative research validates concepts and designs before significant development resources are invested. Ongoing research monitors how products are used in the wild and identifies opportunities for optimization. Each type serves different purposes and informs different kinds of decisions.

Information architecture (IA) addresses how information is structured, labeled, and organized to support usability and findability. Good IA creates intuitive pathways through complex systems, helping users understand where they are, what they've found, what's available, and how to get where they want to go.

Key Components of Information Architecture

- Organizational structures
- Labeling systems
- Navigation systems
- Search systems

Simple applications with limited functionality may require minimal architectural consideration, but complex platforms with diverse user types, numerous features, and extensive content demand thoughtful structural design. Poor information architecture manifests in user complaints about getting lost, inability to find features, confusion about how different parts of a system relate to each other, and general feelings of being overwhelmed. These symptoms often emerge gradually as products evolve, making it important for product managers to recognize architectural debt just as they would technical debt.

For product managers, understanding IA principles helps in making strategic decisions about product structure. Should a new feature be integrated into an existing workflow or presented as a standalone tool? Should related functions be grouped by user role, task type, or some other logic? How will users discover new capabilities as the product evolves? IA frameworks provide the conceptual tools for answering these questions thoughtfully.

Interaction design focuses on the moment-by-moment exchanges between users and products. It defines not just what a product does, but how it communicates and responds to user actions. Effective interaction design creates experiences that feel natural, efficient, and satisfying. Central concerns of interaction design include;

- **Affordances and signifiers** – Ensuring users understand interactive elements

- **Feedback and response times** – Providing immediate system responses

- **Error prevention and recovery** – Reducing user mistakes and enabling easy correction

- **Progressive disclosure** – Showing information only when needed

- **Input methods** – Designing for diverse user inputs (touch, voice, keyboard, etc.)

The nuances of interaction design have profound effects on user satisfaction and efficiency. Consider how different users respond to error messages that blame them ("You entered an invalid email") versus those that accept responsibility ("We couldn't recognize that email format") or offer constructive guidance ("Please include the symbol in your email address"). Consider how response times shape user perceptions—delays under 0.1 seconds feel instantaneous, while those exceeding 1-second interrupt flow and require feedback to maintain user confidence. These details may seem trivial in isolation but collectively determine whether using a product feels frustrating or fluid.

For product managers, interaction design considerations directly impact user satisfaction and efficiency. A product might offer powerful functionality, but if its interaction design is poor, it requires too many clicks, providing inadequate feedback, or using confusing terminology users will struggle to access that value.

Conversing fluently with UX designers about interaction design enables product managers to balance business requirements with usability considerations.

Visual design within UX goes beyond aesthetics to support usability, reinforce branding, establish hierarchy, and create emotional connections. While visual design often receives disproportionate attention in product discussions (it's what stakeholders can see most easily), experienced product managers understand that it works alongside other UX disciplines rather than standing alone. Effective visual design in UX considers;

- **Visual hierarchy** – Guiding user attention
- **Consistency and patterns** – Creating intuitive interfaces
- **Accessibility** – Ensuring inclusivity for all users
- **Brand alignment** – Reflecting company identity
- **Emotional design** – Evoking appropriate user responses

The strategic importance of visual design is often underestimated. Visual elements communicate subtle messages about product quality, attention to detail, and brand values. They establish an emotional tone and influence user trust. They guide attention and help users prioritize information. They play a crucial role in accessibility, determining whether products can be used effectively by people with visual impairments or cognitive limitations. Product managers who relegate visual design to mere decoration miss opportunities to leverage design as a strategic differentiator.

For product managers, visual design decisions carry strategic weight. The visual treatment of a product influences how users perceive its quality, trustworthiness, and suitability for their needs. It affects whether users focus on the most important functionality or get distracted by secondary elements. And it determines whether the product feels cohesive or fragmented as new features are added over time.

Implementation and Evaluation

Usability evaluation provides empirical evidence about how well a product meets user needs. It offers a reality check against assumptions and reveals opportunities for improvement. Usability evaluation ranges from quick, informal tests to rigorous lab studies. Several usability evaluation methods help assess and improve user experience:

Usability Testing: This method involves observing real users as they interact with the product to identify usability problems, measure task success rates, and collect qualitative feedback. It helps determine how intuitive and efficient the product is in real-world scenarios.

Heuristic Evaluation: Experts review the product based on established usability heuristics (such as Nielsen's usability principles) to detect usability issues without requiring user testing. This method is cost-effective and can be conducted early in the design process.

Cognitive Walkthrough: This technique simulates a new user's thought process while performing tasks, evaluating whether they can complete the task easily without prior experience. It is useful for identifying potential learning curve issues.

Accessibility Evaluation: This assessment ensures the product is usable by individuals with disabilities by testing against accessibility guidelines like WCAG. It considers various impairments, such as visual, auditory, motor, and cognitive disabilities, ensuring inclusivity.

Benchmark Testing: This method compares usability metrics (e.g., task completion time, error rates) against industry standards or competitors to gauge product performance. It helps set usability goals and track improvements over time.

The timing and approach to usability evaluation should vary based on product stage and specific objectives. Early-stage products benefit from frequent, lightweight evaluations focused on validating fundamental concepts and identifying major usability issues. Mature products may require more specialized evaluation targeting specific user segments or particular aspects of the experience. Critical applications—those where usability failures could have serious consequences—often warrant more rigorous evaluation approaches with larger sample sizes and controlled testing environments.

Accessibility evaluation deserves particular attention as both an ethical imperative and, increasingly, a legal requirement. Products should be evaluated against established accessibility guidelines (such as the Web Content Accessibility Guidelines) to ensure they can be used effectively by people with diverse abilities. This includes considerations for visual, auditory, motor, and cognitive impairments. For product managers, prioritizing accessibility isn't just about compliance or avoiding legal risk—it's about expanding market reach and building products that truly work for all users. For product managers, usability evaluation serves multiple purposes throughout the product lifecycle, including;

Concept Validation (Early Stage):

Testing low-fidelity prototypes and wireframes helps assess the viability of design ideas before committing to development.

Feedback from potential users guides initial design decisions and prevents costly rework later.

Pre-Release Testing:

Identifying critical usability issues in beta testing allows teams to fix major flaws before product launch.

Gathering insights into user satisfaction and ease of use ensures a positive launch experience.

Post-Release Optimization:

Continuous usability testing with real users helps refine the product based on actual usage patterns and feedback.

Regular updates and iterative improvements keep the product relevant and user-friendly.

UX practitioners create various deliverables to document and communicate research findings, design concepts, and implementation requirements such as;

Personas: Fictional user profiles representing different segments of the target audience, detailing user demographics, behaviors, motivations, and pain points. These help teams design solutions that meet specific user needs.

Customer Journey Maps: Visual representations showing how users interact with the product across different touchpoints, highlighting frustrations and opportunities for improvement.

User Flows: Diagrams mapping out the steps users take to accomplish tasks, helping identify inefficiencies or unnecessary complexities in workflows.

Wireframes: Low-fidelity sketches outlining the product's layout and interface structure, providing a basic visual representation before detailed design work begins.

Prototypes: Interactive models allowing stakeholders and testers to experience the product's functionality before development, enabling early feedback and iteration.

Design Systems: A collection of reusable UI components, design guidelines, and patterns ensuring consistency and scalability across the product's ecosystem.

The format and fidelity of UX deliverables should align with their specific purpose and audience. Conceptual artifacts like personas and journey maps help build a shared understanding of user needs and pain points across diverse stakeholders. Structural artifacts like sitemaps and user flows communicate how different parts of a product relate to each other. Visual artifacts like wireframes and prototypes make abstract ideas concrete and facilitate feedback. Each serves different purposes at different stages of product development.

The emergence of design systems represents a significant evolution in how UX deliverables support product development. Rather than creating designs from scratch for each new feature or product, organizations increasingly invest in comprehensive systems of reusable components, patterns, and guidelines. These systems promote consistency across products, accelerate design and development cycles, and reduce the cognitive load on both designers and users. For product managers, design systems offer a way to balance innovation with stability—providing frameworks within which new ideas can flourish without reinventing fundamental interactions.

For product managers, these deliverables provide valuable reference points throughout the product development process. Personal and journey maps inform feature prioritization by highlighting which user needs are most critical. User flows identify opportunities to streamline common tasks. Wireframes and prototypes facilitate stakeholder alignment before expensive development begins. And design systems support scalable growth by establishing patterns that can be applied consistently as products evolve.

UX work doesn't happen in isolation—it must integrate with broader product development processes. This integration takes different forms depending on organization size, development methodology, and product complexity. In agile environments, UX practitioners often work one or two sprints ahead of development, conducting research and creating designs that will be implemented in upcoming iterations. In larger organizations with waterfall approaches, UX research and design might constitute distinct phases before development begins. Regardless of methodology, effective integration requires thoughtful coordination.

Successful integration depends on both process considerations and interpersonal dynamics. On the process side, it's important to establish clear handoffs, feedback mechanisms, and decision points that accommodate both UX and development workflows. Equally important are the interpersonal aspects—building shared understanding and mutual respect between UX practitioners, developers, and product managers. This requires deliberate effort to bridge different professional languages, priorities, and ways of thinking about problems and solutions.

For product managers, key considerations for UX integration include timeline alignment, shared understanding, decision authority, and success metrics. Product managers often serve as bridges between UX teams and other stakeholders, translating user insights into business value and advocating for appropriate UX investment. This bridging function requires understanding both

UX methodologies and business constraints, a balancing act that defines modern product management.

The Strategic Value of UX

UX investment delivers measurable business value across multiple dimensions. Understanding this value helps product managers advocate for appropriate UX resources and processes within their organizations. Research consistently shows that effective UX contributes to increased conversion rates, enhanced customer retention, reduced support costs, accelerated development, premium pricing potential, and positive brand perception.

The return on investment (ROI) for UX initiatives can be substantial but often requires thoughtful measurement approaches. Some benefits manifest directly in short-term metrics, increased conversion rates on redesigned forms, reduced call center volume after usability improvements, and higher feature adoption following interaction refinements. Others emerge more gradually or indirectly improved brand perception leading to word-of-mouth growth, reduced development costs through earlier problem identification, and enhanced employee satisfaction through pride in well-designed products. Product managers should work with UX practitioners to establish appropriate success metrics that capture both immediate impacts and longer-term strategic benefits.

Industry research provides compelling evidence for UX investment. Studies have shown that companies with strong UX capabilities outperform their peers in stock performance, customer satisfaction, and development efficiency. Every dollar invested in

UX brings between $2 and $100 in return, according to various studies. These aggregate findings help make the case for UX investment broadly, but organization-specific data is often more persuasive to senior stakeholders. Building a library of internal case studies where UX improvements deliver measurable business results can be a powerful tool for securing ongoing support.

For product managers, articulating this business value is essential when competing for resources or justifying UX-driven decisions. By connecting UX improvements to specific business outcomes This design change increased trial conversions by 15%" product managers can build organizational support for user-centered approaches.

The UX field continues to evolve in response to technological advancements, changing user expectations, and shifts in how products are developed and deployed. Staying informed about these trends helps product managers anticipate new opportunities and challenges. Current trends reshaping the UX landscape include AI and machine learning integration, voice and conversational interfaces, augmented and virtual reality, inclusive design, design ethics, and continuous research operations.

The integration of artificial intelligence into UX practice represents perhaps the most significant current evolution. AI impacts UX in at least three distinct ways. First, it creates new interaction possibilities, from conversational interfaces to predictive features that anticipate user needs. Second, it offers new tools for UX practitioners themselves—research analysis that identifies patterns in large datasets, design systems that generate variations based on parameters, and evaluation tools that automate certain types of testing. Third, it raises new ethical questions about transparency, agency, bias, and the appropriate balance between automation and human control. Product managers must navigate these dimensions thoughtfully, leveraging AI's benefits while mitigating its risks.

Beyond AI, other technological trends continue to expand UX beyond traditional screen-based interactions. Voice interfaces eliminate visual interfaces for some interactions. Augmented and virtual reality blend digital and physical worlds in immersive experiences. Haptic feedback adds tactile dimensions to digital interactions. These modalities don't replace traditional interfaces but complement them, creating new possibilities for more natural, contextual, and embodied user experiences. Product managers should monitor these developments with an eye toward how they might address specific user needs or enable new product capabilities.

For product managers, these trends represent both opportunities and challenges. They open new possibilities for delivering value but also raise the bar for what constitutes an acceptable user experience. Navigating this evolving landscape requires continuous learning and close collaboration with UX specialists who track developments in their field.

Social and ethical dimensions of UX have gained increased attention as digital products play ever-larger roles in society. Concerns about digital well-being have prompted questions about features that might promote addiction or unhealthy usage patterns. Privacy concerns have highlighted the importance of transparent data practices and user control. Accessibility has evolved from a specialized consideration to a mainstream requirement. And the potential for design to manipulate or deceive users has sparked debates about ethical boundaries in persuasive design. Product managers increasingly need frameworks for making decisions that balance business objectives with broader social responsibilities.

Product managers need not become UX experts to work effectively with UX professionals, but developing UX literacy pays dividends. This literacy enables more productive collaboration, more informed decision-making, and ultimately, better products. Practical steps for building UX literacy include observing research sessions, learning basic UX terminology, practicing design thinking methods, staying informed about UX trends, and building relationships with UX practitioners.

Observing actual users interacting with products, whether through formal usability tests or informal field studies provides particularly valuable education for product managers. These direct observations cut through assumptions and theoretical debates, revealing how users think about and use products in practice. They highlight the gap between intended and actual use, reveal unexpected pain points, and generate empathy that influences future decision-making. Making time for regular user observation, despite busy schedules, distinguishes product managers who truly understand their users from those who merely claim to.

The most effective product managers recognize that UX literacy isn't just about acquiring knowledge—it's about adopting a mindset that values user perspectives and empirical evidence. This mindset influences not just how products are designed but how requirements are gathered, how success is measured, and how decisions are made throughout the product lifecycle.

Understanding the UX landscape equips product managers to create products that don't just function well but truly meet user needs in meaningful ways. By embracing user-centered principles, leveraging appropriate research methodologies, and collaborating effectively with UX specialists, product managers can drive the development of products that stand out in crowded markets.

The relationship between product management and user experience continues to evolve, with boundaries between the disciplines increasingly blurring. Many product managers now incorporate UX techniques directly into their work, while UX practitioners increasingly understand business constraints and technical limitations. This convergence reflects a shared recognition that great products emerge from balancing user needs, business goals, and technical feasibility—a balance that defines both modern UX practice and effective product management.

As digital products become increasingly central to how people work, learn, connect, and access essential services, the importance of thoughtful user experience only grows. Product managers who invest in understanding the UX landscape position themselves to create products that don't merely compete in existing markets but define new standards for how technology serves human needs. In doing so, they fulfill the highest purpose of product management: creating solutions that genuinely improve people's lives.

CHAPTER 3
DECODING THE PRODUCT MANAGEMENT ROLE A COMPREHENSIVE EXPLORATION

Product Management is a dynamic and multifaceted discipline that sits at the crucial intersection of business, technology, and, most importantly, user experience. It's the art and science of strategically guiding a product through its entire lifecycle, from the initial spark of an idea, through rigorous development and testing, to its successful launch, subsequent growth and maturity, and eventual, inevitable decline. A Product Manager (PM) acts as the central conductor of this complex orchestra, expertly orchestrating diverse teams and stakeholders to transform an often-nebulous product vision into a tangible, marketable reality. This chapter provides an in-depth exploration of the world of product management, meticulously outlining the core responsibilities, essential skills, unique perspectives, and daily challenges that drive successful product development. For UX professionals, a comprehensive and nuanced understanding of these elements is not just beneficial, it's absolutely crucial for fostering effective collaborations with PMs, building strong working relationships, and contributing meaningfully to the entire product development process.

The fundamental responsibility of a PM can be distilled into defining the "why," "what," and "when" of a product. They are the voice of the customer, the astute market analyst, the strategic visionary, and the driving force behind execution, all encapsulated within a single, demanding role. This broad and encompassing scope necessitates a highly diverse skillset, spanning analytical thinking and in-depth market research to exceptional communication, effective leadership, a solid foundation in technical proficiency (though not necessarily deep coding skills), and a genuine passion for understanding user needs. A PM must be comfortable navigating the inherent ambiguities of product development, making informed, data-driven decisions, often with limited information and under tight deadlines, and skillfully influencing outcomes without necessarily wielding direct authority over every team involved.

Product Strategy: Laying the Foundation for Success

At the very core of product management lies the critical element of product strategy. This is the overarching and comprehensive plan that defines the product's long-term vision, identifies and segments the target audience, and establishes its unique and compelling competitive positioning within the market. A well-defined and robust product strategy provides clear answers to a set of fundamental questions: What specific problem are we aiming to solve for our users? Who exactly are our target users, and what are their specific needs, pain points, motivations, and behaviors? What are our key differentiators that set us apart from the competition and provide a unique value proposition? And finally, how will we effectively measure the success of our product, both in terms of user adoption and business impact? The product strategy acts as a reliable compass, consistently guiding all subsequent product development efforts. It serves as a unifying force, ensuring that every individual and team involved is working harmoniously towards a shared and clearly defined goal, and that the product seamlessly aligns with the overall business strategy and overarching objectives. A PM plays a pivotal role in not only developing but also effectively communicating the product strategy, ensuring it's clearly understood and fully embraced by all stakeholders involved. This often involves conducting rigorous market research, thoroughly analyzing competitor offerings, identifying unmet user needs and emerging opportunities, and synthesizing this information into a cohesive and actionable plan.

Market Analysis: Understanding the Playing Field and Identifying Opportunities

A truly successful product is one that deeply resonates with its target market. Therefore, a profound and nuanced understanding of the market is essential for any PM. This involves conducting thorough market research, carefully analyzing market trends, and identifying potential opportunities for growth and expansion, as well as potential threats to the product's success and long-term viability. PMs must possess a keen awareness of the competitive landscape, understand the strengths and weaknesses of their direct and indirect competitors. They need to be adept at identifying emerging trends, technological advancements, and shifts in user behavior, and proactively anticipating how these factors might impact the product and its future trajectory. This market intelligence serves as a crucial input to the product strategy, helps prioritize features based on market demand and user needs, and guides product positioning within the competitive landscape to ensure maximum impact. UX professionals can significantly contribute to this vital process by providing valuable insights into user behavior, preferences, pain points, and unmet needs, gleaned from user research, usability testing, and other user-centered design methodologies.

Product Roadmapping: Charting the Course and Managing Expectations

Once the product strategy is clearly defined and the market landscape is understood, the PM takes the lead in creating a comprehensive product roadmap. This roadmap is a high-level visual representation of the product's planned development over a specific period, typically spanning several months or even years. The roadmap outlines key features, planned releases, important milestones, and anticipated timelines, providing a clear and concise picture of the product's future direction and anticipated evolution. It serves as an invaluable communication tool, keeping stakeholders informed about the product's progress, planned developments, and anticipated timelines. It's important to remember that the roadmap is not a static document set in stone; rather, it's a living document that evolves and adapts as new information becomes available, priorities inevitably shift, and market conditions change. A PM must be flexible and adaptable, demonstrating a willingness to adjust the roadmap as needed to respond to changing market conditions, valuable user feedback, emerging technological advancements, or shifts in business strategy. UX professionals can actively contribute to the roadmapping process by effectively advocating for user-centric features, ensuring that usability considerations are thoroughly incorporated into the development plan, and providing data-driven insights to support prioritization decisions.

Stakeholder Management: Navigating the Complex Network of Interests

Product development is inherently a team sport. It involves close collaboration with a diverse range of stakeholders, each with their own unique perspectives, priorities, and interests. These stakeholders can include engineers, designers, marketers, sales teams, customer support, senior management, and even external partners. A PM sits at the center of this complex network, bearing the responsibility for managing stakeholder expectations, aligning diverse perspectives, and ensuring that everyone is aligned and working towards the same common goals. This requires strong communication, negotiation, and influencing skills. PMs must be able to clearly and concisely articulate the product vision, effectively explain product decisions, often justifying them with data and user insights, and address stakeholder concerns in a timely and professional manner. They need to build strong and trusting relationships with stakeholders, fostering a culture of open communication, transparency, and collaborative problem-solving. UX professionals are key stakeholders in the product development process, and effective communication between UX and PM is absolutely crucial for overall product success. This collaboration ensures that user needs are understood, prioritized, and effectively translated into product features.

Product Lifecycle Management: From Inception to Obsolescence and Beyond

A product's journey doesn't simply end with its launch. It goes through various stages, from introduction and growth to maturity and eventual decline. A PM manages the product throughout its entire lifecycle, from its initial inception to its eventual obsolescence. This involves closely monitoring product performance post-launch, actively gathering user feedback through various channels, and making informed decisions about future development, enhancements, and iterations. PMs need to analyze data from various sources, identify areas for improvement, and prioritize new features and enhancements based on user needs, market demands, and business objectives. They also need to make difficult but necessary decisions about when to retire a product, sunset features, or invest in new iterations and versions. Understanding the product lifecycle is crucial for making informed decisions about product strategy, resource allocation, long-term product viability, and ensuring the product continues to meet evolving user needs and market demands.

The PM Perspective and Priorities: A UX Perspective for Effective Collaboration

Understanding the PM's perspective and priorities is essential for UX professionals to collaborate effectively, build strong working relationships, and maximize their impact on the product development process. PMs are often juggling multiple competing priorities, balancing user needs with business constraints, technical feasibility, time-to-market pressures, and resource limitations. They are responsible for delivering products on time and within budget; while also ensuring they meet user expectations and achieve business objectives. They need to make data-driven decisions, often with limited information and under tight deadlines. UX professionals can significantly help PMs by providing valuable user insights, effectively advocating for user-centric design principles, and demonstrating the value of UX through data and metrics. By understanding the PM's challenges, constraints, and priorities, UX professionals can become invaluable partners in the product development process, contributing to a more user-centered, market-driven, and ultimately successful product. Open communication, mutual respect, and a shared understanding of the product vision are essential for a productive and impactful UX-PM partnership.

CHAPTER 4
ALIGNING UX AND BUSINESS GOALS A SYMBIOTIC RELATIONSHIP FOR SUSTAINABLE SUCCESS

In today's dynamic and fiercely competitive market, User Experience (UX) has transcended its traditional role as a mere design consideration and emerged as a critical driver of business success. A strategically crafted UX approach is no longer a luxury but a necessity, directly impacting key business metrics, from heightened conversion rates and diminished customer churn to fortified brand loyalty and amplified customer lifetime value. This chapter delves deep into the intricate and symbiotic relationship between UX and business goals, illustrating how the seamless integration of these two seemingly distinct realms can unlock substantial value, propel organizational growth, and ensure sustainable success.

Deconstructing the Interconnectedness: Beyond Surface Level Design

The conventional perspective often relegated UX to a design function, operating in isolation from core business objectives. This antiquated viewpoint is fundamentally flawed and increasingly detrimental. UX is not solely about aesthetics, visual appeal, or surface-level usability; it's about cultivating a profound understanding of your users – their intricate needs, underlying motivations, inherent behaviors, and persistent pain points – and meticulously crafting experiences that not only resonate deeply with them but also seamlessly align with and contribute to the achievement of overarching business goals. Envision it as a two-sided coin: one side representing the nuanced needs and desires of the user, and the other side embodying the strategic aspirations and measurable objectives of the business. A truly successful UX strategy harmonizes these two seemingly disparate sides, forging a mutually beneficial, win-win scenario where user satisfaction and business growth become intertwined and mutually reinforcing.

Quantifying the Business Value of UX: Beyond Intuition and Anecdotes

The impact of UX on tangible business outcomes is not merely anecdotal or based on gut feeling; it's substantiated by a wealth of data and rigorous research. Numerous studies have consistently demonstrated a strong and positive correlation between exceptional user experiences and demonstrably improved business performance across various industries and sectors. Here are some key areas where a strategic focus on UX can directly and measurably contribute to the attainment of critical business goals:

Elevated Conversion Rates: Turning Browsers into Buyers

A frictionless, intuitive, and engaging user journey can significantly and demonstrably boost conversion rates. By streamlining the user experience, eliminating friction points that impede progress, and strategically guiding users towards desired actions (e.g., completing a purchase, subscribing to a newsletter, downloading a resource), UX can directly and positively impact the bottom line, driving revenue growth and profitability.

Mitigating Customer Churn: Fostering Loyalty and Retention

Frustrating, confusing, or cumbersome experiences can lead to customer churn, eroding your customer base and impacting long-term profitability. A well-designed UX strategy prioritizes the creation of positive, memorable, and valuable interactions, fostering customer satisfaction, cultivating brand loyalty, and significantly reducing the likelihood of customers abandoning your product or service in favor of competitors.

Strengthening Brand Loyalty: Cultivating Advocates and Brand Ambassadors

Exceptional and consistent user experiences contribute significantly to building a positive and enduring brand perception. When users have enjoyable, seamless, and valuable interactions with your product or service, they are far more likely to become loyal customers, repeat buyers, and enthusiastic advocates for your brand, spreading positive word-of-mouth and driving organic growth.

Maximizing Customer Lifetime Value (CLTV): A Long-Term Perspective

By increasing customer retention rates, fostering brand loyalty, and encouraging repeat purchases, UX indirectly but powerfully contributes to a higher Customer Lifetime Value. Happy, satisfied, and engaged customers are more likely to make repeat purchases, engage with your brand over a longer period, and contribute to sustained revenue generation, ultimately maximizing their value to the business.

Reducing Support Costs: Empowering Self-Service and Minimizing Frustration

A well-designed UX can proactively minimize the need for extensive customer support. Intuitive interfaces, clear and concise instructions, and readily available self-service resources can empower users to resolve issues independently, reducing the burden on your support team, freeing up valuable resources, and minimizing operational costs.

Gaining a Competitive Edge: Differentiating in a Crowded Marketplace

In an increasingly competitive and saturated marketplace, a superior and demonstrably better user experience can be a significant and sustainable differentiator. By offering a more enjoyable, efficient, and valuable experience than your competitors, you can effectively attract and retain customers, gaining a crucial competitive edge and positioning your brand for long-term success.

Frameworks and Techniques for Seamless Alignment: Bridging the Gap

Successfully aligning UX efforts with overarching business strategy requires a structured, methodical, and data-driven approach. Here are some essential frameworks and techniques that can facilitate this critical alignment:

Deeply Understanding Business Objectives: Setting the Foundation

The crucial first step involves clearly and comprehensively defining the organization's core business goals. What are the key performance indicators (KPIs) that the business is striving to improve? Are you primarily focused on increasing revenue, expanding market share, enhancing customer acquisition, or improving overall customer satisfaction? A thorough understanding of these objectives is paramount for effectively aligning UX efforts and ensuring they directly contribute to the achievement of strategic priorities.

Conducting Comprehensive User Research: Knowing Your Audience

A deep, nuanced, and data-driven understanding of your target audience is essential for creating truly effective and impactful user experiences. Invest in conducting thorough user research to gain insights into their specific needs, underlying motivations, inherent behaviors, and persistent pain points. This research can encompass a variety of methodologies, including user interviews, surveys, usability testing, A/B testing, and data analytics.

Developing Detailed User Personas: Humanizing Your Users

Based on the insights gleaned from your user research, create detailed and representative user personas that embody your target audience segments. These personas should comprehensively represent your ideal users, including their demographics, professional backgrounds, personal goals, technological proficiency, and key frustrations. Personas help to humanize your users, ensuring that your UX efforts are laser-focused on their specific needs and preferences.

Mapping User Journeys: Visualizing the Experience

Visualize the various steps that users take when interacting with your product or service, from initial awareness to post-purchase engagement. Mapping these user journeys helps to identify potential pain points, areas of friction, and opportunities for improvement. It also ensures that the user experience is consistent, seamless, and enjoyable across all touchpoints and channels.

Prioritizing UX Initiatives: Focusing on High-Impact Activities

Not all UX initiatives are created equal. It's critical to prioritize the initiatives that will have the most significant and measurable impact on achieving your business goals. Utilize a framework like the MoSCoW method (Must have, should have, could have, Won't have) to prioritize UX projects based on their importance to business objectives, feasibility, and available resources.

Establishing Metrics and Measurement: Tracking Progress and Demonstrating ROI

Define clear, measurable, and relevant metrics to track the success of your UX initiatives and demonstrate their return on investment (ROI). These metrics should be closely aligned with your overarching business goals. For example, if your primary goal is to increase conversion rates, you might track metrics such as click-through rates, add-to-cart rates, and purchase completion rates.

Fostering Collaboration and Communication: Breaking Down Silos

Effective collaboration and transparent communication between UX designers, business stakeholders, product managers, and developers are absolutely essential for successfully aligning UX and business goals. Regular meetings, shared documentation, collaborative workshops, and open feedback channels can help to ensure that everyone is on the same page, working towards common objectives.

Integrating UX into the Business Culture: A Holistic Approach

Aligning UX and business goals is not a one-time project or a tactical initiative; it's an ongoing, continuous process that requires a fundamental shift in organizational culture. Organizations that truly and authentically embrace UX understand that it's not just a department, a set of tools, or a series of design sprints; it's a way of thinking, a core value that permeates every aspect of the business. They prioritize user-centricity in all facets of their operations, from product development and marketing to customer service and internal processes. The seamless alignment of UX and business goals is not merely a best practice or a desirable objective; it's a strategic imperative for organizations that aspire to thrive and achieve sustainable growth in today's increasingly competitive and customer-centric landscape. By deeply understanding the intricate interconnectedness of UX and business objectives, diligently utilizing appropriate frameworks and techniques, and fostering a genuine user-centric culture, organizations can unlock significant value, measurably improve business performance, and cultivate lasting, mutually beneficial customer relationships. Investing in UX is not simply an expense; it's a strategic investment in the future of your business, a commitment to creating products and services that not only meet and exceed user expectations but also drive business growth, enhance brand reputation, and ensure long-term success. It's about building a sustainable competitive advantage by creating exceptional experiences that resonate with users, build loyalty, and drive business value.

CHAPTER 5
USER RESEARCH THE FOUNDATION OF UX AND PM

In UX, user research is integral to crafting intuitive and enjoyable digital experiences. It allows designers to understand how users interact with interfaces, identify usability issues, and refine designs to improve efficiency and satisfaction. In product management, user research plays a crucial role in defining product strategies, prioritizing features, and ensuring that every decision aligns with user needs and business goals. Ultimately, user research minimizes the risk of failure by validating ideas before significant investments in development.

Key Methods of User Research

There are several methods of user research, each offering unique insights. User interviews provide qualitative data by allowing researchers to engage directly with users, gathering rich insights into their motivations, challenges, and expectations. Surveys enable data collection at scale, helping teams identify trends and patterns across a broader user base. Usability testing involves observing users as they interact with a product, revealing friction points and areas for improvement. A/B testing compares two versions of a product or feature to determine which performs better based on real user behavior. Ethnographic studies provide contextual insights into how users interact with products in their natural environments. Focus groups gather multiple users for discussions, uncovering shared perspectives and challenges. Diary studies track user interactions over time, revealing long-term patterns and behaviors.

User research informs product decisions at every stage of the product development lifecycle. During the ideation phase, it identifies market gaps and user pain points, guiding the development of features that address real needs. In the design phase, it ensures that interfaces are intuitive and user-friendly. Through development and testing, user feedback helps refine the product before launch. Even after launch, continuous research helps optimize products based on evolving user needs and behaviors. Without this iterative feedback loop, products can quickly become outdated or misaligned with user expectations, leading to churn and reduced engagement.

Validating design choices through user research is essential for creating successful products. Often, designers and product managers have assumptions about what users want, but these assumptions can be misleading. By conducting user research, teams can test hypotheses, gather empirical data, and make informed decisions. This reduces the likelihood of building features that users do not find valuable or intuitive. Additionally, research allows for iterative improvements, enabling teams to make small, incremental changes based on user feedback rather than undertaking costly redesigns later.

Beyond validation, user research is a key driver of product innovation. Understanding user behaviors and needs often uncovers opportunities for new features, services, or entirely new products. Many groundbreaking innovations have emerged from insights gathered through user research. For instance, companies like Airbnb, Netflix, and Amazon continuously rely on user research to enhance their offerings, creating personalized experiences that keep users engaged and satisfied. Companies that ignore the power of user research often struggle to maintain relevance and fail to capitalize on market trends driven by real user demands.

User research is not just about improving usability but also about ensuring business success. A product that aligns user needs is more likely to achieve higher adoption rates, improved customer retention, and positive word-of-mouth marketing. Companies that prioritize user research gain a competitive advantage by building products that stand out in crowded markets. Furthermore, user research fosters customer-centricity, shifting the focus from internal assumptions to real-world user needs. Products that fail to incorporate user research risk becoming redundant or ineffective, leading to wasted resources and lost revenue.

Challenges and Best Practices in User Research

While user research is invaluable, it must be conducted effectively to yield meaningful insights. Some challenges include ensuring a representative sample, balancing qualitative and quantitative analysis, and integrating research into the product development workflow. If research participants do not reflect the actual user base, findings may be skewed. Over-reliance on one research method can lead to incomplete insights, so companies must adopt a mixed-method approach. Additionally, research should be a continuous process, not a one-time activity. Successful companies embed user research throughout the product lifecycle, ensuring continuous feedback collection, iterative design improvements, and adaptability to changing user needs.

User research extends beyond individual products to broader business strategies. Insights from user research can inform marketing strategies, ensuring that communication resonates with target audiences. It can also lead to customer support improvements by addressing common user pain points and identifying new product opportunities. Businesses that actively conduct user research foster a culture of continuous improvement, enabling them to adapt quickly to evolving market demands.

One of the most significant benefits of user research is its ability to foster empathy within teams. When designers, developers, and product managers understand the real struggles of users, they are more likely to create solutions that genuinely address those pain points. Empathy-driven design leads to more meaningful user experiences, which, in turn, drive customer loyalty and long-term engagement. Moreover, user research contributes to accessibility and inclusivity by ensuring that products cater to diverse user groups, including people with disabilities, older users, and individuals from various cultural backgrounds. Inclusive design not only broadens a product's reach but also aligns with ethical and regulatory standards, enhancing a brand's reputation and social impact.

Some organizations overlook user research due to time and budget constraints. However, cost-effective research techniques can provide valuable insights without excessive spending. These include guerrilla testing, which involves quick and informal usability tests in real-world environments, online surveys to gather broad user feedback at scale, and moderated usability sessions that conduct focused user testing with minimal resources. Companies that recognize the importance of continuous user research and allocate resources accordingly will ultimately build more successful and user-friendly products.

The Future of User Research

As technology advances, user research methodologies continue to evolve. Emerging trends include artificial intelligence and machine learning for sophisticated data analysis and user behavior predictions, eye-tracking studies to understand how users visually interact with digital products, sentiment analysis to gauge user emotions based on feedback and interactions, and behavioral analytics to provide deeper insights into user actions and preferences. Additionally, remote research tools make it easier than ever to gather feedback from global audiences, allowing for a more diverse and representative understanding of user behavior.

User research is a cornerstone of both UX and product management. It provides the insights necessary to create user-centered products that solve real problems, improve usability, and drive business success. By leveraging methods such as user interviews, surveys, usability testing, and A/B testing, teams can validate ideas, refine designs, and foster innovation. Companies that prioritize continuous user research gain a deeper understanding of their audience, leading to better decision-making, higher user satisfaction, and sustain competitive advantage in the market. Ultimately, investing in user research is not just about improving products, it is about building a culture that values user needs and continuously strives to meet them.

CHAPTER 6
COLLABORATION STRATEGIES FOR UX AND PM

The journey of crafting a successful product is a collaborative endeavor, a symphony of diverse talents orchestrated by the harmonious partnership between User Experience (UX) and Product Management (PM). While both teams share the overarching ambition of delivering a valuable and user-friendly product, their domains and methodologies can sometimes create friction. This chapter delves into the intricacies of fostering effective collaboration between UX and PM teams, emphasizing the vital roles of communication, transparency, and mutual respect. By embracing and implementing these strategies, organizations can unlock the synergistic potential of both teams, paving the way for innovative and user-centric products that resonate with their target audience.

Before embarking on the path to effective collaboration, it's crucial to establish a shared understanding of each team's distinct yet interconnected roles. Product Management (PM) typically focuses on the "what" and "why" of the product. They are the architects of the product vision, strategy, and roadmap, meticulously prioritizing features based on a confluence of market analysis, business goals, and a deep understanding of user needs. They serve as the voice of both the customer and the business, balancing user desires with market realities and business objectives.

User Experience (UX), on the other hand, concentrates on the "how" of the product. They are the champions of the user, meticulously designing intuitive and engaging interfaces that not only meet user needs but also seamlessly solve their problems. They are the voice of the user, advocating for their needs and ensuring their experience is at the forefront of the product development process.

Recognizing these distinct yet intertwined roles is the foundational step towards cultivating effective collaboration. PMs rely on UX's expertise to understand user behavior, conduct user research, and create user-centered solutions that truly resonate with the target audience. Conversely, UX depends on PM's strategic vision, market insights, and business acumen to ensure their designs align with overarching business objectives and contribute to the product's overall success.

The roles of UX and PM have evolved significantly over the past decade. Traditionally, UX designers focused primarily on interface aesthetics, while PMs concentrated on feature lists and business requirements. Today, these roles have expanded and overlapped in many ways, creating both opportunities and challenges for collaboration.

Modern UX professionals are now expected to have a deeper understanding of business contexts and technical constraints. They incorporate research methodologies, data analysis, and strategic thinking into their design process. Similarly, contemporary PMs are increasingly expected to understand user-centered design principles, participate in user research, and advocate for the user experience as a core business value.

This evolution has blurred the lines between the two disciplines, making collaboration both more essential and more complex. Organizations that recognize this shifting landscape and adapt their collaboration models accordingly gain a significant competitive advantage.

Spotify provides an excellent example of clearly defined yet collaborative UX and PM roles. Their "squad" model groups small, cross-functional teams around specific product areas. Within each squad, PMs (called "Product Owners" in their Agile framework) focus on defining the problem space and business objectives, while UX designers concentrate on solving these problems through user-centered design.

What makes their model successful is the explicit recognition of overlapping responsibilities coupled with clear accountability. PMs are ultimately accountable for what gets built and why, while UX is accountable for how it gets built. However, both actively participate in each other's domains: designers contribute to product strategy, and PMs participate in design critiques.

This mutual involvement fosters respect and understanding while maintaining clear lines of responsibility, preventing the confusion that can arise when roles are too fluid or too rigidly separated.

Building Bridges: Strategies for Effective Collaboration

Effective collaboration isn't built overnight; it's a continuous process that requires nurturing and commitment from both teams. Open and consistent communication forms the bedrock of this collaborative relationship. Establishing regular communication channels, such as daily stand-ups to quickly align progress and address any roadblocks, weekly meetings to delve deeper into strategic discussions and review progress against milestones, and shared communication platforms like Slack or Microsoft Teams to facilitate ongoing dialogue and information sharing, are essential.

Creating a culture that encourages open dialogue, active listening, and constructive feedback is paramount. Both teams must feel comfortable sharing their ideas, expressing concerns, and challenging assumptions without fear of judgment. This requires fostering a safe and inclusive environment where diverse perspectives are valued and respected.

Transparency and shared understanding are equally vital. Information should flow freely between the two teams. PMs should proactively share the product roadmap, providing context on upcoming features and their rationale, along with market research data, user feedback, and business goals with the UX team. This transparency empowers UX to understand the bigger picture and design solutions that align with the overall product strategy.

Similarly, UX should share user research findings, design iterations, prototypes, and usability testing results with the PM team. This ensures PMs are aware of user needs and preferences, enabling them to make informed decisions about product direction and prioritization. A shared understanding of the user, the market, and the business context is crucial for both teams to work in unison.

Mutual respect and trust are the cornerstones of any successful partnership. Recognizing and appreciating the unique value each team brings to the table is essential. Avoid creating silos and instead foster a culture of collaboration where both teams work together as equal partners, each contributing their expertise to the shared goal. This requires acknowledging that both teams have different perspectives and priorities and finding ways to bridge those differences through open communication and compromise.

While the importance of communication is often emphasized, implementing structured frameworks that systematize this communication can significantly enhance collaboration. The RACI model (Responsible, Accountable, Consulted, Informed) can be adapted specifically for UX-PM collaboration. For each key deliverable or decision point in the product development process, clearly define who is responsible for the work, accountable for decisions, consulted before actions are taken, and informed after decisions are made.

Decision journals document not just what was decided, but why and how decisions were made. When shared between UX and PM teams, these journals create a valuable record of the thought process, constraints, and trade-offs that informed key product decisions. Each entry should include the decision needed, options considered, evaluation criteria, final decision and rationale, assumptions made, expected outcomes, and validation metrics.

Establishing consistent rituals creates predictable touchpoints between UX and PM teams. Monday vision sessions align goals and priorities for the week, mid-week collaborative work periods tackle complex problems together, and end-of-week retrospectives reflect on what worked and what could be improved. These rituals create a rhythm that enables both structured and spontaneous collaboration, preventing the common scenario where teams only interact when problems arise.

Leveraging collaborative tools and techniques can significantly streamline workflows and facilitate communication. Joint workshops, where both teams come together to brainstorm ideas, define user needs, and prioritize features, provide a platform for collaborative problem-solving and consensus building. Shared documentation platforms, such as Confluence or Google Docs, serve as a central repository for all project-related information, ensuring everyone has access to the latest updates and reducing the risk of miscommunication.

The Opportunity Canvas is a powerful tool that brings UX and PM perspectives together. It includes sections for user problems and needs (UX focus), business objectives and success metrics (PM focus), market context and competitive landscape (shared focus), and proposed solutions and approaches (collaborative output). When completed jointly, this canvas ensures both teams understand and contribute to the product opportunity from multiple angles. Rather than having separate user personas created by each team, develop unified personas that incorporate both user experience needs and business/market considerations. These comprehensive personas serve as a shared reference point that both teams can use to guide their work and communication.

Traditional product roadmaps often focus heavily on features and timelines—primarily PM concerns. Experience roadmaps, by contrast, map out how the user experience will evolve, incorporating both feature releases and experience improvements. This hybrid approach creates a shared vision that both teams can rally behind, ensuring that neither business goals nor user experience considerations are neglected in planning. Regular feedback sessions, scheduled throughout the product development lifecycle, provide opportunities for both teams to provide and receive feedback on designs, prototypes, and features. This iterative feedback loop ensures the product evolves in a way that meets both user needs and business goals.

When collaboration breaks down or products don't meet expectations, conducting blameless postmortems helps teams learn without assigning fault. These sessions focus on systemic issues rather than individual actions, identifying opportunities to improve processes and communication.

Establish a practice where UX reviews PM deliverables (like product requirements) and PM reviews UX deliverables (like design specifications). This cross-functional review process helps identify misalignments early and builds mutual understanding of each other's work.

While not always feasible, co-locating UX and PM teams can significantly enhance communication and collaboration. Proximity fosters informal interactions, facilitates quick problem-solving, and strengthens team bonds.

In today's increasingly remote work environment, creating virtual equivalents of co-location becomes crucial: virtual war rooms for real-time collaboration, always-on video portals creating a sense of shared space, digital whiteboarding for visual collaboration, and informal virtual hangouts for relationship building. These approaches help recreate the spontaneous interactions that naturally occur in physical workspaces, which are often where the most valuable collaborations begin.

Strategic Alignment and Shared Ownership

Early involvement of UX in the product development process is critical. Instead of treating UX as an afterthought, integrating them from the very beginning allows their expertise to inform the product strategy and direction. This proactive approach ensures user needs are considered from the outset, preventing costly rework later in the development cycle. Early UX involvement also empowers them to conduct thorough user research, understand user behaviors, and develop user-centered solutions that truly address their needs.

Aligning both teams with shared metrics and goals creates a sense of shared ownership and purpose. Defining key performance indicators (KPIs) that reflect both user satisfaction, such as Net Promoter Score (NPS) or user engagement metrics, and business success, such as revenue growth or market share, ensures both teams are working towards the same objectives. This shared focus fosters a collaborative environment where both teams are invested in the overall success of the product.

The dual-track development model, where discovery and delivery activities occur simultaneously but are tightly integrated, provides an excellent framework for UX-PM collaboration. The discovery track, led jointly by UX and PM, focuses on understanding problems, exploring solutions, and validating ideas before they enter the delivery pipeline. The delivery track focuses on building and shipping validated solutions. This approach ensures that both teams are involved throughout the product lifecycle, with clear responsibilities at each stage. It prevents the common problem where PM hands requirements to UX, who then hands design to Engineering, with limited collaboration between stages.

Intuit's "Design for Delight" (D4D) methodology illustrates how closely integrated UX and PM can drive significant business results. Their approach emphasizes three principles: deep customer empathy where both UX and PM participate in customer research; going broad to go narrow with collaborative ideation sessions; and rapid experiments with customers through quick iterations of prototypes. This methodology has become central to Intuit's product development process and has contributed to the company's continued growth and customer loyalty. The key to its success is that it creates a shared framework that both UX and PM teams use to guide their work, rather than separate methodologies for each discipline.

Traditional product metrics often favor business outcomes (conversion rates, revenue) or technical outcomes (performance, scalability). Implementing a balanced scorecard approach ensures that user experience metrics receive equal weight in decision-making. A balanced scorecard might include business metrics (revenue, conversion), experience metrics (satisfaction scores, task completion rates), efficiency metrics (development time, iteration cycles), and learning metrics (insights generated, hypotheses validated). By measuring and reporting on all four dimensions, organizations ensure that both UX and PM priorities remain visible and valued.

Empathy and User-Centricity

Empathy and a deep understanding of the user are paramount. Both UX and PM should champion the user and cultivate a user-centric mindset. Encourage both teams to develop empathy for the user by conducting user research, creating user personas to represent target user groups, and engaging in user testing to understand their needs, frustrations, and motivations. A shared focus on user-centricity will naturally bring the teams closer together, fostering a sense of shared purpose and driving them to create products that truly resonate with their target audience.

One of the most powerful ways to build shared empathy is through joint field research, where PM and UX teams visit users together in their natural environments. This shared experience creates a common reference point that both teams can draw upon in future discussions. Rather than having UX conduct research and report findings to PM, or having each team conduct separate research, joint sessions ensure that both perspectives are present during the observation and interpretation phases. This prevents the common scenario where research findings are filtered through the lens of one discipline before reaching the other.

Regular empathy-building exercises can help maintain a user-centric focus: role-playing sessions where team members act out user scenarios, "a day in the life" simulations where teams attempt to use their product for real-world tasks, empathy maps created collaboratively to explore what users think, feel, say, and do, and user journey mapping exercises that trace the emotional and functional aspects of user experiences. These exercises are most effective when PM and UX teams participate together, creating shared understanding that informs both strategic and design decisions.

Create systems that make user feedback and research findings accessible to everyone, not just those who participated in the research: user feedback dashboards that aggregate and categorize user feedback from multiple channels, research repositories where all user studies are documented and searchable, and regular insight-sharing sessions where both teams discuss recent learnings about users. This democratization ensures that user insights remain at the center of all decisions, regardless of which team is leading a particular initiative.

Organizational Support and Culture

While much of this chapter focuses on tactics that UX and PM teams can implement themselves, organizational support plays a crucial role in fostering effective collaboration.

Executive leadership must demonstrate commitment to UX-PM collaboration through unified messaging about the importance of both disciplines, balanced resource allocation that recognizes the value of both functions, performance evaluations that reward collaborative behaviors, and organizational structures that facilitate rather than hinder collaboration. When leadership sends mixed signals or implicitly values one function over the other, even the best-intentioned collaboration efforts will struggle to succeed.

Organizations should invest in cross-training opportunities that help each discipline understand the other: PM-focused workshops for UX professionals that cover business modeling, market analysis, and prioritization frameworks; UX-focused workshops for PMs that cover design thinking, usability principles, and research methodologies; and joint workshops that develop shared skills like facilitation, conflict resolution, and collaborative problem-solving. This cross-pollination of skills not only improves collaboration but also makes each team more effective in their core responsibilities.

Creating a culture that values collaboration requires consistent reinforcement: recognition programs that highlight successful collaborations, success stories that demonstrate the impact of effective UX-PM partnerships, physical and digital spaces designed to facilitate cross-functional interaction, and hiring practices that screen for collaborative mindsets in both disciplines. Culture is shaped by what organizations celebrate and reward, so ensuring that collaborative successes receive visibility is essential for long-term change.

Overcoming Common Challenges

Despite the best intentions, UX-PM collaboration often faces recurring challenges. Acknowledging these challenges and developing specific strategies to address them is essential for sustainable collaboration.

Timeline pressure is one of the most common sources of friction between UX and PM teams. When deadlines loom, the thoughtful process of user research and design iteration can seem like a luxury. Strategies to address this challenge include time-boxed research and design approaches that scale to fit available timelines, research and design patterns that can be adapted from previous work, parallel workflows where research for future features happens alongside design for current features, and clear prioritization frameworks that help both teams make thoughtful trade-offs under pressure. The key is developing approaches that maintain the spirit of user-centered design and strategic thinking even when timelines are compressed, rather than abandoning these principles entirely.

In many organizations, UX and PM functions report through different management chains, creating potential alignment challenges: UX might report through Design, Technology, or a dedicated UX organization, while PM typically reports through Product organizations, sometimes with dotted lines to Marketing or Technology. These reporting structures can create competing priorities and incentives. Strategies to navigate these dynamics include joint OKRs or goals that span organizational boundaries, regular alignment meetings between leadership of both functions, explicit discussion of organizational tensions and how to manage them, and escalation paths for resolving conflicts that balance both perspectives. Recognizing that organizational politics are real and developing explicit strategies to navigate them prevents these factors from undermining day-to-day collaboration.

Even when collaboration is strong, UX and PM will sometimes have legitimately different priorities: PM may need to prioritize a quick-win feature for business reasons, even if it's not the ideal user experience, while UX may advocate for addressing fundamental usability issues before adding new features. Rather than treating these tensions as failures of collaboration, successful teams develop frameworks for openly discussing and resolving priority conflicts: value vs. effort matrices that incorporate both business and user experience factors, RICE frameworks (Reach, Impact, Confidence, Effort) that quantify different types of value, MoSCoW prioritization (Must have, Should have, Could have, Won't have) with input from both perspectives, and explicit trade-off discussions that acknowledge both short and long-term implications. The goal isn't to eliminate differences in perspective—which would undermine the value of having distinct disciplines—but to develop healthy ways of resolving these differences when they arise.

Measuring Collaborative Success

How do organizations know if their UX-PM collaboration efforts are working? Establishing metrics for collaborative success is essential for continuous improvement.

Process metrics focus on how teams work together: cycle time from concept to launch to determine if collaborative processes are streamlining or slowing delivery, rework frequency to track how often designs or requirements need significant revision, research utilization to measure how frequently user research is cited in product decisions, and cross-functional participation to assess what percentage of each team's meetings include the other team. These metrics help identify where collaboration processes may need refinement.

Outcome metrics focus on the results of collaboration: user satisfaction with new features to determine if collaboratively developed features are more successful, first-time success rates to measure if users can successfully use new features without assistance, business goal achievement to assess if products meet their business objectives, and team satisfaction surveys to evaluate if both teams feel their perspectives are valued. These metrics help validate whether improved collaboration is actually leading to better products.

IBM's Enterprise Design Thinking framework includes a "Loop Measurement" approach that assesses how well teams are collaborating across disciplines. Their assessment includes "Hills" (are teams aligned around common goals?), "Playbacks" (do teams regularly share and critique work together?), and "Sponsor Users" (do teams maintain ongoing relationships with representative users?). Organizations can adapt this type of framework to create a baseline assessment of their current UX-PM collaboration and track improvements over time.

The Benefits of Collaboration

Investing in effective collaboration between UX and PM yields significant benefits. Improved product quality is a direct result of combining UX's user-centered design approach with PM's strategic vision. Products developed through effective collaboration typically demonstrate greater user adoption and engagement, higher customer satisfaction and loyalty, more intuitive interfaces with lower support costs, better alignment with market needs and business objectives, and more cohesive experiences across features and touchpoints.

Increased efficiency stems from streamlined workflows, clear communication, and reduced rework. When UX and PM collaborate effectively, design iterations decrease as alignment improves, features are more likely to be built right the first time, handoffs between teams become smoother, decision-making accelerates as shared context grows, and resources are allocated more effectively across priorities.

Enhanced innovation arises from the cross-pollination of ideas and perspectives. The intersection of UX and PM thinking creates a fertile ground for innovation: design solutions benefit from business and market insights, business strategies are enriched by deep user understanding, novel approaches emerge from the combination of both perspectives, teams become more willing to experiment and take calculated risks, and products differentiate more effectively from competitors.

Stronger team morale develops from a collaborative environment that fosters a sense of community and shared purpose: professional growth accelerates through cross-disciplinary learning, work satisfaction increases as teams see the full impact of their contributions, relationships strengthen through shared successes and challenges, retention improves as team members value their collaborative environment, and recruitment becomes easier as word spreads about the positive culture.

Adobe's transformation from a traditional software company to a cloud-based subscription business required a fundamental shift in how their UX and PM teams worked together. They implemented many of the collaborative approaches described in this chapter, including joint discovery processes that brought UX and PM together at the earliest stages, shared metrics that balanced business and experience outcomes, regular design sprints that involved cross-functional participation, and user feedback mechanisms that were accessible to both teams. The results were impressive: faster time-to-market, higher user satisfaction scores, increased subscription retention, and ultimately, significant business growth. This transformation demonstrates how UX-PM collaboration can drive not just product improvements but fundamental business outcomes.

In conclusion, effective collaboration between UX and PM is not just a desirable attribute; it's a fundamental requirement for creating successful products in today's competitive market. By implementing the strategies outlined in this chapter, organizations can break down silos, foster mutual respect, and unlock the full potential of both teams.

The result will be a more user-centric product development process, leading to improved product quality, increased efficiency, enhanced innovation, and stronger team morale. Ultimately, a strong UX and PM partnership is a win-win for everyone – the users, the business, and the teams themselves. It's the foundation upon which successful products are built.

As the product landscape continues to evolve and user expectations rise, the ability to seamlessly integrate business strategy and user experience becomes an increasingly powerful competitive advantage. Organizations that invest in cultivating this collaborative capability will find themselves better positioned to navigate market changes, respond to user needs, and deliver products that truly stand out in crowded marketplaces.

The journey toward effective collaboration is ongoing—there is no perfect end state, only continuous improvement. By remaining committed to the principles of open communication, mutual respect, shared goals, and user-centricity, UX and PM teams can build lasting partnerships that drive success far beyond what either could achieve alone.

CHAPTER 7
PRODUCT ROADMAPS AND PRIORITIZATION

In the evolving landscape of product development, few challenges match the complexity of deciding what to build next. Product teams find themselves at the intersection of competing demands: user needs calling for attention, business goals requiring advancement, technical debt demanding resolution, and market opportunities beckoning exploration. Amid these pressures, road mapping and prioritization emerge not merely as scheduling exercises but as the strategic backbone that transforms vision into reality through deliberate choices about resource allocation.

The Strategic Foundation of Product Roadmaps

A product roadmap represents far more than a timeline of feature releases. At its core, it serves as a strategic communication tool that articulates how a product will evolve to deliver increasing value to users while advancing business objectives. Effective roadmaps bridge the chasm between high-level strategy and ground-level execution, creating alignment across diverse stakeholders with different perspectives, timescales, and concerns. They provide the crucial connective tissue between the "why" of product strategy and the "what" of feature development.

The central challenge of road mapping stems from its inherently dual nature. Roadmaps must simultaneously provide enough clarity to guide immediate work while maintaining sufficient flexibility to adapt to inevitable change. This tension becomes particularly acute in rapidly evolving markets where competitive landscapes shift unpredictably, user expectations continuously evolve, and technological capabilities advance at an accelerating pace. Too rigid a roadmap becomes obsolete before implementation; too flexible a roadmap fails to provide meaningful guidance. Navigating this balance requires roadmaps structured around multiple time horizons with corresponding levels of commitment and detail.

The near-term horizon, typically spanning one to three months, contains specific, committed features with clear implementation plans. At this level, teams need precise scope definition, technical specifications, and delivery timelines to coordinate efficient execution. The mid-term horizon, generally covering three to twelve months, outlines initiatives with defined objectives but flexible implementation details. This allows teams to maintain strategic direction while adapting tactical approaches based on learnings from current work. The long-term horizon, extending beyond twelve months, captures broader strategic directions and market opportunities without committing to specific solutions. This provides navigational guidance while acknowledging the impossibility of predicting exact feature requirements far in advance.

Modern road mapping approaches increasingly organize around themes, problems to solve, or outcomes to achieve rather than specific features. This shift from output-focused to outcome-focused planning acknowledges a fundamental truth: features themselves matter less than the user and business outcomes they enable. A theme-based roadmap might be organized around objectives like "Simplify the onboarding experience," "Expand monetization options," or "Reduce support volume" rather than listing specific features. This approach maintains strategic coherence while creating space for teams to discover optimal solutions through user research and experimentation.

Outcome-based roadmaps also facilitate more productive stakeholder conversations. Rather than debating the relative merits of specific features, discussions center on which outcomes matter most and how success will be measured. This reframes roadmap negotiations from subjective preference battles to evidence-based deliberations about which outcomes will deliver the greatest value to users and the business. It also creates natural alignment points between product development and broader organizational objectives, helping teams articulate how their work contributes to company-level goals.

The Art and Science of Prioritization

The process of translating strategic direction into an actionable roadmap inevitably confronts the central challenge of product development: prioritization. With limited resources and unlimited possibilities, teams must make difficult tradeoffs about what to build now, what to build later, and what not to build at all. These decisions grow particularly challenging because they involve balancing different types of value (immediate user needs versus long-term strategic positioning), different stakeholder perspectives (engineering priorities versus sales requests), and different time horizons (quick wins versus foundation-building investments).

Without structured approaches to prioritization, decisions often default to implicit and problematic patterns. The "squeaky wheel" pattern prioritizes whatever generates the most noisily-typically requests from vocal customers, aggressive salespeople, or insistent executives. The "recency bias" pattern gives disproportionate weight to the latest feedback or market development rather than consistent patterns over time. The "consensus" pattern attempts to please everyone by saying yes to everything, inevitably leading to overcommitment and under delivery. These unstructured approaches not only produce suboptimal decisions but create organizational friction as teams perceive the process as arbitrary or political.

Effective prioritization frameworks provide structure for evaluating options systematically, though no framework can eliminate subjectivity entirely. What these frameworks offer is a common language for discussing tradeoffs, consistent evaluation criteria that reduce bias, and transparency that builds trust in the decision-making process. Several frameworks have emerged to address this challenge, each with particular strengths for specific contexts.

Value-based prioritization assesses initiatives by quantifying their potential impact on key metrics relative to implementation costs. Teams estimate the expected value gain across dimensions like engagement, revenue, or satisfaction, then compare this against implementation complexity to calculate return on investment. This approach requires defining clear success metrics for each initiative and gathering data to forecast potential impact. The strength of value-based approaches lies in their direct connection to measurable outcomes, though they require robust measurement capabilities and can struggle with initiatives whose impact occurs across multiple metrics or over extended timeframes.

The RICE scoring model provides a systematic framework that incorporates multiple dimensions of value and feasibility. RICE stands for Reach (how many users will this impact), Impact (how much will it affect each user), Confidence (how certain are we about these estimates), and Effort (how much work is required). By multiplying Reach, Impact, and Confidence, then dividing by Effort, teams generate a score that balances potential value against implementation cost while accounting for uncertainty. This balanced approach prevents teams from overinvesting in high-effort, low-impact features while acknowledging the inherent uncertainty in forecasting feature impact.

The Cost of Delay framework focuses on the opportunity cost of postponing initiatives. By quantifying how much value is lost for each week or month of delay, teams can sequence work to maximize cumulative value delivery over time. This approach proves particularly valuable when comparing initiatives with different value and time profiles. An initiative that delivers moderate value quickly might outrank one with higher total value but significant development time when evaluated through a Cost of Delay lens. This time-sensitive approach helps teams identify "thin slices" of larger initiatives that can deliver partial value sooner rather than waiting for complete implementation.

Jobs-to-be-Done prioritization centers on understanding the fundamental tasks users hire the product to accomplish. This approach identifies underserved jobs with high importance to users, focusing development on filling significant gaps in current solutions. By mapping the competitive landscape against critical jobs, teams identify opportunities where meaningful differentiation can create competitive advantage. This deeply user-centered approach ensures development efforts connect directly to genuine user needs rather than speculative feature ideas, though it requires substantial upfront research to identify and validate the job landscape.

Balancing Competing Priorities and Timeframes

The most challenging aspect of prioritization involves balancing fundamentally different types of work that resist direct comparison. Customer-facing features deliver visible improvements that users can immediately appreciate, while technical foundation work creates infrastructure that enables future capabilities. The danger of continually deferring technical work in favor of visible features is accumulating "technical debt" that eventually cripples development velocity. Similarly, teams must balance creating new capabilities against refining existing ones through reliability improvements, performance optimization, and usability enhancements.

Perhaps the most difficult is balancing immediate market demands against longer-term strategic positioning. Short-term features typically address known user needs with predictable value, while strategic initiatives position the product for future opportunities with less certain but potentially larger returns. Teams that exclusively focus on immediate needs may deliver steady incremental improvement while missing transformative opportunities or emerging market shifts.

A balanced approach allocates capacity across different work categories rather than exclusively prioritizing one type. Many product teams adopt explicit investment ratios that dedicate specific percentages of development capacity to different work categories. A common pattern allocates 60-70% to customer-facing enhancements, 20-30% to platform and infrastructure improvements, and 10-20% to exploration and innovation work. These allocations vary by product maturity, market conditions, and technical circumstances, but the principle remains: deliberate investment across work categories ensures continued progress on multiple fronts while preventing any single concern from monopolizing resources.

The execution of prioritized initiatives through road mapping faces several common pitfalls that undermine effectiveness. The feature factory trap occurs when teams measure success by feature delivery rather than user outcomes. This leads to bloated products filled with underutilized capabilities that increase complexity without proportional value. To counter this tendency, teams must maintain relentless focus on outcome metrics, continuously evaluating whether delivered features actually achieve their intended effects.

The certainty illusion manifests when roadmaps project false precision about delivery timelines and feature details, especially for distant initiatives. This creates unrealistic expectations that inevitably lead to disappointment when reality intrudes. Effective roadmaps acknowledge increasing uncertainty with time horizons, using broader time ranges and less detailed specifications for distant initiatives. Many teams adopt progressive elaboration approaches that maintain rough outlines for distant work while continuously refining near-term initiatives as implementation approaches.

Solution fixation happens when teams become attached to specific implementations before thoroughly understanding the underlying problems. This prematurely narrows exploration and often leads to suboptimal outcomes as teams rush to build solutions before validating their necessity. Problem-first road mapping counters this tendency by explicitly separating problem definition from solution development, ensuring a thorough exploration of user needs before committing to specific features.

The overcommitment syndrome reflects teams' chronic tendency to underestimate implementation complexity while overestimating available capacity. This results in missed deadlines, scope reduction, and team burnout as reality forces painful adjustments. Data-driven capacity planning helps teams develop more realistic estimates based on historical performance, while buffer allocation creates schedule room for inevitable unexpected complications. Some teams deliberately plan only 70-80% of theoretical capacity, recognizing that emergent work will consume the remainder through production issues, urgent customer needs, or discovery of necessary technical work.

While strategic thinking matters more than tools, several practical approaches help teams create more effective roadmaps. Opportunity solution trees visually connect strategic objectives to potential solution options, helping teams maintain line-of-sight between daily work and overall direction. This approach encourages exploring multiple solution paths for each opportunity rather than prematurely committing to a single implementation. Now-next-later maps group initiatives by relative timing rather than specific dates, reducing false precision while maintaining directional clarity. This approach acknowledges increasing uncertainty with time horizon while still communicating sequence and priority.

Confidence labeling explicitly marks the certainty level of different roadmap elements, distinguishing between committed work, likely directions, and exploratory possibilities. This creates appropriate expectations across stakeholders and prevents provisional plans from being misinterpreted as promises. Assumption tracking documents the key beliefs underlying roadmap decisions, creating checkpoints for validating or invalidating these assumptions as new information emerges. By making assumptions explicit, teams create natural triggers for roadmap adjustments when foundational beliefs prove incorrect.

Different stakeholders require different presentations of roadmap information to be maximally useful. Executive leadership needs strategic themes connected to business outcomes and market positioning, with less emphasis on implementation details. Sales and marketing require clarity on upcoming capabilities to set appropriate customer expectations, with a particular focus on timing and differentiation points. Development teams need technical context and implementation sequencing to plan dependencies and resource allocation effectively.

Rather than creating a single roadmap document, effective product teams maintain a central roadmap repository that generates appropriate views for different audiences. Each view presents the information relevant to that audience while maintaining consistency with the master plan. This approach recognizes that roadmaps serve different purposes for different stakeholders: strategic alignment for executives, expectation setting for customers, coordination for development teams, and prioritization guidance for product managers.

When communicating roadmaps externally to customers or partners, additional care is required to balance transparency with flexibility. External roadmaps should focus on problems being solved rather than specific features, avoiding precise dates that create expectation management challenges. Many teams adopt thematic roadmaps for external communication, showing general direction without committing to specific implementations. When timing information is necessary, quarter-based or season-based ranges provide useful guidance while maintaining implementation flexibility. Most importantly, external roadmaps should communicate their provisional nature, helping customers understand that plans represent current intent rather than contractual commitments.

Product prioritization continues to evolve as emerging practices reshape how teams approach these challenges. Continuous discovery replaces periodic planning cycles with ongoing exploration of user needs and solution opportunities. This approach integrates discovery work directly into delivery cycles, creating tighter feedback loops between learning and building. Rather than planning features for months, teams continuously identify potential opportunities, run lightweight experiments to validate solutions, and then feed validated approaches into development. This approach maintains strategic direction through outcome-based objectives while allowing tactical flexibility in solution approaches.

The shift toward autonomous teams with aligned objectives moves from centralized roadmaps to team-level autonomy within clearly defined outcome boundaries. Rather than receiving predefined feature lists, teams receive clear objectives and success metrics, with the freedom to determine the best approaches for achieving these outcomes. This model increases organizational adaptability by pushing decision-making closer to user and technical knowledge while maintaining coherence through shared objectives. It also increases team motivation by connecting directly to purpose and impact rather than feature completion.

Experimentation-driven prioritization replaces upfront estimation with systematic validation through small experiments. Teams prioritize learning opportunities rather than features, developing lightweight tests to validate assumptions before committing to full implementation. This approach acknowledges the inherent uncertainty in predicting feature impact and seeks to reduce this uncertainty through direct evidence. By framing work as experiments rather than commitments, teams create space for learning and adjustment rather than forcing premature certainty.

Dynamic resource allocation moves from fixed team structures to more fluid approaches that reallocate capacity based on evolving priorities. This creates organizational agility to respond to emerging opportunities or changing market conditions. Rather than annual planning cycles that lock resources into predetermined initiatives, this approach enables continuous rebalancing as teams learn which areas deliver the greatest value. This doesn't mean constant reorganization, but rather deliberate capacity management that follows value discovery.

Product road mapping and prioritization exist at the intersection of art and science. The science comes from structured frameworks, quantitative analysis, and evidence-based decision-making. The art involves balancing competing stakeholder needs, navigating uncertainty, and maintaining strategic focus amid constant tactical pressures. The most effective product leaders embrace both dimensions, building rigorous processes for gathering and evaluating evidence while recognizing that human judgment remains essential for interpreting this evidence in context.

The true measure of effective prioritization isn't predictive accuracy but value delivery over time. Teams inevitably make prioritization mistakes - overvaluing some opportunities and undervaluing others. What distinguishes great teams isn't perfection in initial prioritization but their ability to learn and adjust based on actual outcomes. By treating prioritization itself as a product to be refined through feedback and iteration, teams develop increasingly effective approaches tailored to their specific context and challenges.

In the complex reality of product development, perfect roadmaps and prioritization remain aspirational rather than achievable. The best product teams don't let this inherent messiness paralyze them but embrace disciplined approaches that improve decision quality while maintaining adaptability. They recognize that priorities will change as markets evolve, user needs emerge, and technical realities intrude. Rather than fighting this reality, they build processes that accommodate change while maintaining enough stability for efficient execution. In this balance lies the art of transforming infinite possibilities into focused action that steadily advances both user and business value.

CHAPTER 8
MEASURING UX SUCCESS AND ROI

Building on the established metrics and methodologies, organizations need a structured approach to implement ongoing UX measurement. A successful UX measurement program requires clear ownership, consistent processes, and organizational integration. The first step involves designating responsibility for UX measurement. While UX researchers often lead this effort, cross-functional collaboration with analytics teams, product managers, and business analysts creates a more comprehensive view. This collaborative approach also helps integrate UX metrics with broader organizational dashboards rather than creating isolated measurement systems.

Establishing measurement cadence is equally important. Some metrics warrant daily or weekly tracking (like conversion rates or task completion times), while others (such as customer satisfaction or brand perception) might follow quarterly or annual assessment cycles. This cadence should align with product development cycles, ensuring that measurement informs each iteration.

Tool selection represents another critical consideration. The marketplace offers numerous specialized UX research and analytics platforms—from Hotjar and FullStory for behavioral insights to UserZoom and UserTesting for structured research. These specialized tools complement general analytics platforms like Google Analytics or Mixpanel. The ideal toolkit balances comprehensive data collection with practical implementation constraints.

Finally, successful implementation requires documented processes for data collection, analysis, and reporting. These processes should define when measurements occur, who analyzes the data, how insights get distributed, and what actions result from the findings. Documentation ensures consistency even as team members change and creates institutional knowledge around UX measurement practices.

A mature UX measurement program also integrates with existing business processes and reporting cycles. Rather than creating parallel systems, UX metrics should appear alongside financial, marketing, and operational data on executive dashboards and quarterly business reviews. This integration reinforces the connection between user experience and business outcomes while ensuring UX data influences strategic decisions.

Training and enablement represent another crucial element of implementation. Even the best measurement frameworks falter without skilled practitioners who understand both the technical aspects of data collection and the nuanced interpretation of results. Organizations should invest in developing these capabilities through formal training, mentorship programs, and communities of practice where measurement specialists can share knowledge and refine methodologies.

Overcoming Common UX Measurement Challenges

Despite the best intentions, organizations frequently encounter obstacles when attempting to measure UX success. Acknowledging and addressing these challenges proactively improves measurement effectiveness.

Data silos present a significant barrier, with user information often fragmented across marketing analytics, product usage data, customer support records, and sales databases. Breaking down these silos requires both technical solutions (like unified customer data platforms) and organizational changes (cross-functional data sharing agreements). The goal isn't necessarily centralization but rather creating connections between relevant data sources.

Attribution challenges also complicate UX measurement. When multiple changes occur simultaneously—interface updates alongside marketing campaigns or pricing changes—isolating the impact of UX improvements becomes difficult. Controlled experimentation helps address this challenge, as does staggered implementation that allows for clearer before-and-after comparisons.

Sample bias represents another common pitfall. Organizations often collect data from the most engaged users while missing insights from those who abandoned the product or never adopted it. Comprehensive measurement requires reaching beyond current users to understand the experiences of non-users and former users, often through targeted research rather than passive analytics.

Resource constraints frequently limit measurement ambitions. When facing limited budgets or personnel, organizations should prioritize a few high-impact metrics rather than attempting comprehensive measurement. Starting with clear business priorities helps focus limited resources on the most valuable insights.

Finally, privacy considerations increasingly impact data collection practices. With regulations like GDPR and CCPA restricting data gathering, organizations must balance measurement needs with compliance requirements. This often means focusing on anonymous or aggregated data and being transparent with users about how their information informs product improvements.

Organizational skepticism presents another significant challenge, particularly in environments where data-driven decision making isn't well established. Some stakeholders may question the validity of UX metrics or resist implementing changes based on user research findings. Addressing this skepticism requires both education (helping stakeholders understand measurement methodologies) and demonstration (showing concrete examples where UX improvements drove business results). Starting with small, measurable successes builds credibility for larger measurement initiatives.

Technical debt can also undermine measurement efforts. Legacy systems often lack appropriate instrumentation for capturing detailed user interactions, while fragmented technology stacks create disconnected user journeys that are difficult to track cohesively. Organizations sometimes need to invest in technical infrastructure—implementing proper event tracking, establishing user identity management across touchpoints, or developing APIs between systems—before comprehensive UX measurement becomes possible.

Balancing standardization with flexibility represents another ongoing challenge. While consistent metrics enable benchmarking and trend analysis, different products and features may require specialized measurements. The most effective measurement programs establish core metrics applied universally while allowing teams to supplement these with context-specific indicators that address unique aspects of their user experiences.

Evolving Metrics for Emerging Technologies

As technology landscapes evolve, UX measurement approaches must adapt to new interaction paradigms. Emerging technologies present unique measurement challenges that require innovative metrics and methodologies.

Voice interfaces, for instance, demand different success indicators than graphical interfaces. Traditional task completion rates remain relevant, but metrics like speech recognition accuracy, conversation abandonment points, and natural language understanding success become equally important. Companies like Amazon track "voice shopping conversion rate" to measure how effectively Alexa facilitates purchases compared to screen-based alternatives.

Augmented and virtual reality experiences introduce spatial and physical dimensions to UX measurement. Traditional usability metrics expand to include considerations like spatial awareness, physical comfort during extended use, and presence (the feeling of being immersed in the virtual environment). Companies like Oculus measure "comfort scores" alongside traditional engagement metrics to ensure positive user experiences.

Artificial intelligence introduces another layer of complexity. When systems adapt to individual users, standardized measurement becomes challenging since each user experiences a personalized version of the product. Metrics must evolve to assess both the quality of personalization and the overall system performance. Netflix, for example, measures not just whether recommendations lead to viewings but how recommendation diversity affects long-term engagement.

IoT ecosystems connect multiple devices and touchpoints, requiring holistic measurement approaches that track experiences across devices rather than in isolation. Cross-device completion rates and ecosystem usability scores help organizations understand how effectively users navigate these interconnected experiences.

As these technologies mature, the UX community continues developing specialized measurement frameworks. Organizations venturing into emerging technologies should contribute to these evolving standards through the transparent sharing of measurement approaches and findings.

Conversational interfaces require evaluating dialogue effectiveness beyond simple task completion. Metrics like conversation repair rate (how often users must rephrase requests), sentiment progression (how user sentiment evolves through a conversation), and topic coherence (how logically the system maintains conversation flow) help quantify conversational quality. Companies like Intercom and Drift have pioneered frameworks for evaluating chatbot effectiveness that balance task success with conversational naturalness.

Wearable technology introduces biometric dimensions to UX measurement. Beyond traditional interaction metrics, wearable experiences might be evaluated through physiological indicators like heart rate variability (measuring stress or calmness), galvanic skin response (indicating emotional arousal), or even neural activity through EEG. These approaches enable more objective measurement of emotional and physical responses to experiences that conventional self-reporting might miss. Companies developing health-focused wearables increasingly incorporate these metrics into product development cycles.

Gesture-based interfaces present unique challenges in measuring precision, intuition, and physical effort. Metrics like gesture recognition accuracy, gestural learnability (how quickly users master new gestures), and fatigue indicators help quantify these specialized interactions. Gaming companies like Nintendo have developed sophisticated frameworks for evaluating motion control experiences that balance precision with physical comfort.

As technologies increasingly blend physical and digital realms, metrics must evolve to capture this integration. Phygital experiences that bridge physical and digital environments—require evaluation frameworks that consider physical context alongside digital interactions. Retail companies implementing technologies like smart mirrors or augmented shopping experiences are pioneering measurement approaches that track both digital engagement and in-store behavior changes.

Building a UX-centric Organizational Culture

The ultimate measure of UX success extends beyond metrics and ROI calculations to fundamental organizational transformation. Building a truly UX-centric culture requires systematic changes in how companies operate and make decisions.

Executive sponsorship provides the foundation for cultural change. When leadership consistently references user experience in strategic discussions and allocates resources based on UX insights, the organization naturally prioritizes user-centered approaches. Companies like Apple and Airbnb demonstrate how executive commitment to UX excellence permeates organizational decision-making.

UX education across disciplines strengthens this cultural foundation. When product managers, developers, marketers, and customer support representatives understand UX principles, measurement becomes everyone's responsibility rather than a specialized function. Organizations like IBM have implemented company-wide design thinking training to build this shared understanding.

Incentive alignment ensures that rewards and recognition support UX excellence. When performance evaluations and bonus structures incorporate UX metrics alongside business outcomes, employees naturally prioritize user-centered decisions. This might include factoring customer satisfaction scores into executive compensation or recognizing teams that significantly improve usability metrics.

Democratizing UX data further reinforces cultural transformation. When user insights are accessible throughout the organization—through self-service dashboards, regular insight newsletters, or centralized research repositories—teams naturally incorporate these insights into daily decisions. Companies like Spotify share user research through accessible formats that non-researchers can easily consume and apply.

Finally, patient persistence recognizes that cultural transformation occurs gradually. The most successful organizations implement UX measurement as part of a long-term strategy that builds organizational maturity over years rather than months. This patient approach allows measurement practices to evolve alongside organizational capabilities and user expectations.

By combining effective metrics with cultural transformation, organizations create sustainable competitive advantage through user experience excellence. The measurement approaches outlined throughout this chapter not only demonstrate UX value but also help create organizations fundamentally oriented around user needs and experiences.

Establishing UX champions within different departments creates a network of advocates who reinforce the importance of user-centered approaches. These individuals, whether formally designated or informally, help translate UX principles into language and practices relevant to their specific domains. Engineering champions might focus on incorporating usability testing into development cycles, while marketing champions might emphasize user feedback in campaign planning. This distributed advocacy system extends UX influence beyond dedicated practitioners and creates sustainable cultural momentum.

Creating feedback loops between user insights and strategic planning strengthens organizational commitment to UX excellence. When annual planning processes explicitly incorporate user research findings—whether through dedicated sessions reviewing key insights or by requiring UX validation of proposed initiatives—user needs naturally influence strategic directions. Companies like Intuit have established formal processes where customer problems directly drive innovation through their "Design for Delight" framework, ensuring user needs remain central to product strategy.

The physical environment also plays a role in reinforcing UX culture. Organizations serious about user-centered design often create visible reminders of user needs throughout their workspaces. Persona posters, journey maps displayed in common areas, and dedicated spaces for usability testing make the user experience tangible rather than abstract. When Salesforce designed its offices, it incorporated "customer rooms" where actual customer feedback and journeys remained visible, ensuring user needs to maintain physical presence in the work environment.

Storytelling and narrative development help cement UX value in organizational memory. Beyond quantitative metrics, organizations should cultivate compelling stories that illustrate UX impact. These narratives, whether detailing how research prevented a costly mistake or how design improvements transformed a struggling product, create memorable examples that influence future decisions. Companies like Google have created internal case studies documenting significant UX improvements and their business impact, creating an institutional memory that guides future work.

Cross-functional collaboration rituals further embed UX into organizational routines. When regular ceremonies—like sprint planning, product reviews, or quarterly business assessments—incorporate UX perspectives and metrics, user-centered thinking becomes habitual rather than exceptional. Organizations might establish protocols where new initiatives require user research input or where product launches include UX readiness assessments alongside technical and marketing readiness checks. These systematic touchpoints ensure UX considerations influence decisions at multiple organizational levels.

By implementing these cultural elements alongside robust measurement practices, organizations transform UX from an isolated specialty into a fundamental business approach. This transformation ultimately represents the greatest return on UX investment—creating enterprises that naturally align business success with user needs through every decision and action.

CHAPTER 9
CASE STUDIES UX-PM COLLABORATION IN ACTION

Case Study 1 Streamlining a Complex Enterprise Application

This case study focuses on a large enterprise software company struggling with low user adoption for its flagship application, a complex CRM system. Initially, the UX and Product Management teams operated in silos, with UX focused on aesthetics and usability while Product Management prioritized features and deadlines. This disconnect resulted in a product that, while feature-rich, was difficult to navigate and ultimately underutilized. We'll examine how these teams, initially at odds, recognized the need for collaboration. The narrative will detail the steps taken to establish a shared vision, beginning with collaborative user research involving both UX designers and product managers observing and interviewing actual users. This shared experience fostered empathy and a deeper understanding of user needs. The case study will then explore how they jointly prioritized features, not just based on business value, but also user needs and pain points identified during the research. This led to a more focused roadmap and a more user-centric approach to development. We'll follow the iterative design and development cycles, showcasing how UX and PM worked together to create prototypes, conduct usability testing, and incorporate feedback into subsequent iterations. The case study will showcase the tangible results of this collaboration, such as a 40% increase in user engagement, a 25% reduction in support costs due to improved usability, and a significant boost in customer satisfaction scores. We'll analyze the specific communication strategies employed, including daily stand-up meetings, shared documentation platforms, and regular feedback sessions. We'll also explore the tools utilized for collaborative design and planning, like Figma and Jira, and how they measured the impact of their collaborative efforts through quantitative metrics like task completion rates and qualitative feedback surveys. Crucially, we'll discuss the challenges they faced, like navigating internal politics and overcoming resistance to change from senior management who were accustomed to the old way of working, and how they addressed them through data-driven presentations and pilot programs.

Case Study 2: Building a Successful Startup from the Ground Up

This case study explores the journey of "Innovate Inc.," a tech startup that prioritized UX-PM collaboration from its inception. They were developing a novel mobile application for personalized learning. We'll follow the development of their app, "Learnify," demonstrating how the close partnership between UX and Product Management enabled them to rapidly iterate and adapt to market feedback, a crucial factor in the fast-paced startup environment. The narrative will emphasize the importance of a shared understanding of the target audience, which they achieved through collaboratively creating detailed user personas and user journey maps. These artifacts served as a constant reminder of who they were building for and what their needs were. The case study will then delve into the collaborative creation of the product roadmap, where UX and PM work together to balance user needs with business goals and technical feasibility. We'll see how this collaborative approach facilitated quick pivots when initial user feedback indicated a need for a core feature change. The case study will analyze how this partnership enabled efficient resource allocation, ensuring that design and development efforts were focused on the most impactful features. We'll also explore how the continuous feedback loop between design, development, and user testing, facilitated by a shared passion for the product, allowed them to create a product that resonated strongly with its target market, leading to rapid user growth and successful seed funding. This case study will also highlight the unique challenges faced by startups, such as limited resources, a highly competitive market, and rapid growth, which often lead to organizational changes. We'll see how a strong UX-PM partnership, built on trust and mutual respect, can be instrumental in navigating these hurdles and fostering a culture of innovation and adaptability.

Case Study 3: Transforming a Legacy Product for the Modern User

This case study examines the revitalization of "ConnectPlus," a legacy product within "Global Communications," a well-established telecommunications company. Faced with a declining user base and increasing competition from more modern platforms, the company recognized the urgent need to modernize its offering. We'll explore how the UX and Product Management teams, initially hampered by departmental silos and a "that's how we've always done it" mentality, collaborated to understand the needs of both existing and potential users. The narrative will focus on the process of conducting extensive user research, including surveys, focus groups, and contextual inquiry, and analyzing existing user data to understand usage patterns and pain points. This data informed us of the definition of a new product vision for ConnectPlus, one that aligned with both evolving user expectations and the overall business goals of Global Communications. We'll discuss the challenges of updating a complex system with years of accumulated code while maintaining compatibility with existing infrastructure and minimizing disruption to current users. This required careful planning, phased rollouts, and constant communication with the user base. This case study will highlight the critical importance of effective communication and stakeholder management, as the UX-PM team had to convince various departments, from engineering to marketing, of the need for change. We'll also explore the need for a flexible and adaptable development process, allowing for adjustments based on user feedback and technological advancements. Finally, we'll analyze how they measured the success of the ConnectPlus transformation, including metrics like user retention rates, new user acquisition, increased market share, and improved customer satisfaction scores. The case study will also examine the long-term impact of the transformation on the company's culture, highlighting how the successful collaboration between UX and PM paved the way for a more user-centric approach to product development across the organization.

Cross-Case Analysis: Best Practices and Lessons Learned

This section synthesizes the key takeaways from the preceding case studies, identifying common themes and best practices for successful UX-PM collaboration. We'll delve into the specific strategies and techniques that contribute to positive outcomes, such as establishing shared goals and KPIs from the outset, fostering open and transparent communication through regular meetings and shared platforms, and implementing collaborative workflows that integrate UX and PM throughout the product development lifecycle. We'll also analyze the common pitfalls and challenges encountered in the case studies, such as resistance to change, conflicting priorities, and communication breakdowns, offering practical advice on how to anticipate, avoid, or mitigate these issues. This cross-case analysis will provide a practical framework for readers to apply the lessons learned to their organizations and projects, empowering them to build stronger UX-PM partnerships and achieve greater product success. We'll conclude by emphasizing the ongoing evolution of UX-PM collaboration in response to changing market dynamics, emerging technologies, and evolving user expectations. The importance of continuous learning, adaptation, and a commitment to user-centricity will be highlighted, ensuring that UX and PM teams can effectively collaborate to create products that not only meet business objectives but also delight and empower users.

CHAPTER 10
THE FUTURE OF UX-PM PARTNERSHIP NAVIGATING THE NEXT FRONTIER

As we've explored throughout this book, the relationship between User Experience and Product Management has undergone a remarkable transformation. What began as distinct disciplines with occasional touchpoints has evolved into a deeply integrated partnership that drives modern product development. This final chapter examines not just where this partnership stands today, but where it's headed as technological, organizational, and societal forces continue to reshape our industry.

The traditional model that positioned UX as "user advocates" and PMs as "business representatives" is giving way to a more nuanced reality where both disciplines share accountability for user outcomes and business success. Organizations at the forefront of this evolution have dismantled artificial barriers, creating environments where expertise flows freely between roles. Companies like Figma, Notion, and Spotify demonstrate how this integration leads to more cohesive products that better serve user needs while achieving business objectives.

This boundary dissolution doesn't eliminate specialization but reframes it within a collaborative context. UX professionals continue to bring depth in research methodologies, design principles, and human psychology, while PMs contribute expertise in market dynamics, business modeling, and organizational alignment. The difference lies in how these specialized skills are deployed—not as separate workstreams but as complementary perspectives applied to shared challenges.

AI as Partnership Catalyst

Artificial intelligence represents perhaps the most transformative force shaping the future UX-PM relationship. Far from replacing these professionals, AI is amplifying their capabilities and creating new collaboration models.

For UX teams, AI tools are revolutionizing design processes through generative systems that can produce UI variations, interaction prototypes, and even anticipate accessibility issues. User research is being transformed through AI-powered analytics that can process massive datasets to identify patterns no human researcher could discover independently.

Meanwhile, PMs are leveraging similar technologies to enhance market analysis, feature prioritization, and resource optimization. AI systems can now simulate market responses to potential features, predict development timelines with surprising accuracy, and identify emerging user needs before they become explicit.

The most profound impact is how these tools are reshaping the UX-PM workflow. As AI handles more routine analytical and production tasks, both disciplines are shifting toward higher-order thinking: defining ethical boundaries, interpreting complex patterns, and making nuanced judgments that machines cannot replicate. This shift creates deeper interdependence between UX and PM professionals as they jointly guide these powerful tools toward human-centered outcomes.

Organizations like Google and Microsoft demonstrate this evolution, with their UX and PM teams collaboratively developing frameworks for responsible AI deployment. These frameworks address questions of transparency, accountability, and value alignment that neither discipline could adequately resolve in isolation.

From Products to Ecosystems

The future scope of UX-PM collaboration extends far beyond individual products to encompass entire ecosystems spanning multiple devices, channels, and service models. This expanded scope requires both disciplines to develop new methods for coordinating efforts across increasingly complex systems.

UX professionals must extend their thinking to address cross-device continuity, service design considerations, and ecosystem-wide information architecture. This means designing not just for screens but for comprehensive user journeys that might include voice interfaces, physical touchpoints, and embedded technologies we can barely imagine today.

Product Managers similarly must evolve from feature orchestrators to ecosystem strategists, balancing standardization with customization across diverse offerings. They must develop platform thinking that enables both coherence and innovation across multiple products while managing complex partnership networks.

Companies that have mastered ecosystem thinking demonstrate the power of strong UX-PM alignment. Apple's seamless experience across hardware, software, and services didn't emerge by accident but through deliberate coordination between design and product leadership. Amazon's expansion from e-commerce to entertainment, voice interfaces, and physical retail similarly reflects a unified vision executed through tight UX-PM collaboration.

To navigate this complexity, forward-thinking organizations are adopting systems-thinking approaches borrowed from complex adaptive systems theory. UX and PM teams jointly create experience maps and service blueprints that visualize user journeys across multiple touchpoints, ensuring cohesive experiences despite the underlying complexity.

The Human Element in an Automated Future

Perhaps the most important trend shaping the future UX-PM partnership is the renewed emphasis on human factors in an increasingly automated world. As AI systems handle more routine decisions and operations, distinctly human capabilities become even more valuable.

The UX-PM teams of tomorrow will differentiate through:

Ethical judgment that ensures technology serves human needs rather than exploiting human vulnerabilities

Cultural sensitivity that adapts experiences to diverse global contexts and value systems

Emotional intelligence that recognizes unstated user needs and addresses the full spectrum of human experience

Creative synthesis that combines diverse inputs into novel solutions no algorithm could generate

This human-centered future requires even deeper collaboration between UX and PM professionals. UX brings methodologies for understanding human needs and behaviors, while PM contributes frameworks for aligning these insights with sustainable business models and technological constraints.

Leading organizations are already prioritizing these human elements, not as a counterpoint to technology but as their essential complement. Companies like Patagonia and Headspace demonstrate how products can be both technologically sophisticated and deeply humane when UX and PM teams jointly commit to authentic human values.

Building Organizational Capability

For organizations seeking to thrive in this future landscape, deliberately developing UX-PM collaboration capabilities becomes a strategic imperative. This development requires attention to multiple dimensions:

Structural alignment that positions UX and PM teams to collaborate effectively, whether through dual-track agile processes, integrated product teams, or matrix structures that balance functional excellence with cross-functional coordination.

Talent development focused on "T-shaped professionals" who combine deep expertise in their primary discipline with a broader understanding of adjacent domains. This includes PM professionals with design thinking capabilities and UX professionals with business acumen.

Shared metrics and incentives that encourage joint accountability for both user outcomes and business results, moving beyond function-specific measures to holistic indicators of product success.

Collaboration technologies that facilitate seamless information sharing and decision-making across disciplines, particularly for distributed teams operating across time zones and geographies.

Organizations like Atlassian and Buffer offer instructive examples, with explicit frameworks for UX-PM collaboration embedded in their operating models. These companies don't leave this critical partnership to chance but deliberately nurture it through structural alignment, shared processes, and cultural reinforcement.

Conclusion: The Indispensable Partnership

As we conclude this exploration of the UX-PM relationship, one truth stands out above all the others: this partnership isn't merely beneficial but essential for creating products that meaningfully improve people's lives while building sustainable businesses.

The future will bring new technologies, methodologies, and organizational models, but the fundamental need for complementary perspectives united by shared purpose will remain constant. UX without PM risks creating beautiful experiences disconnected from business realities. PM without UX risks building profitable products that fail to truly serve human needs. Together, they create the possibility of that rare and valuable outcome: products that are both loved by users and viable as businesses.

The organizations that recognize and nurture this partnership investing in the structures, processes, and cultures that enable meaningful collaboration will be best positioned to thrive in the complex landscape ahead. They will create products that don't merely satisfy functional requirements but resonate deeply with human needs, aspirations, and values.

This isn't just good product development; it's the essence of innovation that matters. And in a world facing unprecedented challenges, that's the innovation we need most.

www.ingramcontent.com/pod-product-compliance
Lightning Source LLC
LaVergne TN
LVHW092233110526
838202LV00092B/18